HOW TO SURVIVE MODERN ART

TATE PUBLISHING

HOW TO SURVIVE MODERN ART

SUSIE HODGE

First published 2009 by order
of the Tate Trustees by
Tate Publishing, a division of
Tate Enterprises Ltd,
Millbank, London SW1P 4RG
www.tate.org.uk/publishing

A catalogue record for this book is
available from the British Library

ISBN 978 1 85437 749 4

Distributed in the United States
and Canada by Harry N. Abrams, Inc.,
New York

Library of Congress Control Number:
2009928894

Designed by Untitled

Printed and bound in China by
C&C Offset Printing Co., Ltd.

Mixed Sources
Product group from well-managed
forests and other controlled sources
www.fsc.org Cert no. SGS-COC-003548
© 1996 Forest Stewardship Council
FSC

Front cover, clockwise from top right:
David Hockney, *A Bigger Splash* 1967
(p.101); Henri Matisse, *The Snail* 1953
(p.25); Ron Mueck, *Ghost* 1998 (p.108);
Marcel Duchamp, *Fountain* 1917 (p.49)

Back cover, clockwise from top left:
Barbara Hepworth, *Forms in Echelon* 1938
(p.68); Chris Ofili, *No Woman No Cry* 1998
(p.107); Bridget Riley, *Hesitate* 1964 (p.18);
Carl Andre, *Equivalent VIII* 1966 (p.89);
René Magritte, *Ceci n'est pas une Pipe*
1928–9 (p.66)

Measurements of artworks are given in
centimetres, height before width.

CONTENTS

Modern art can be bizarre or baffling. It can be funny, frivolous or fascinating. Sometimes it can be pretentious, or puzzling, or pointless. But it can also be stimulating, thought-provoking, absorbing and exciting. It can be all of those things – why else would artists think it worth risking everything for? Whatever their reasons for producing art and whatever the meanings behind it, this book aims to give you some answers to the many questions modern art provokes, helping you both to enjoy and understand it better.

TAKING PART

Once photography was invented, what was the point of artists trying to copy the real world? Photography and film can do that so shouldn't art do something different?

Technical skill, such as accurate perspective and tone can be seen, but what about the skill of ideas? Some artists have felt that worrying too much over technique can stifle the imagination.

It's pleasurable to marvel at an artist's dexterity, but some artists can make us think in a whole new way, which is another kind of participation.

We live in a world full of ideas. Modern art has moved forward, opening up new concepts, making us reconsider the world around us.

Art before 1900

Art is always changing. For instance, in Europe before 1500 the Christian Church was extremely powerful and religious subjects dominated what artists produced. Gradually the Church's influence declined and subjects such as portraits, landscapes and historical events became more acceptable. Most artists learned their trade by being apprenticed to older artists, but academies began opening all over Europe and by the 19th century these were the best places to study to be an artist. Students copied art from the past and were taught the accepted rules about what subjects were appropriate and what materials could be used.

When the Industrial Revolution spread wealth across Europe during the late 18th and early 19th centuries, the middle classes began commissioning artists. Between these commissions, artists began producing work they wanted to, even without having buyers. Some abandoned the academies' rules and began exploring their own creative ideas. There was a financial risk if their work was rejected from academy exhibitions, but the freedom of artistic expression was more important to them.

Soon artists also began thinking that it was not necessary to try to copy the world to create art and they began exploring feelings, atmosphere and real people doing everyday things, rather than royalty, the nobility or members of the clergy looking down on the rest of us.

'I know what I like'

Many people still prefer 'realistic' art that they can recognise. Skills that make art appear lifelike are often valued above other creative talents. It's reassuringly familiar, while a lot of modern art can be confusing and difficult to understand. Read the Art in Context box and see what you think.

Aim, point and aspire!

As artists began to experiment, they also spoke to each other about their ideas. Those with similar ambitions sometimes formed movements; groups of artists were often taken more seriously than individuals. Different concepts and materials were tried out and old conventions were cast aside. Throughout the 20th century several art movements formed, broke up and altered as artists' aims changed.

WHAT IS MODERN ART?

'An artist is not a special kind of person.
Every person is a special kind of artist.'
Meister Eckhart

Piet Mondrian, *The Tree A* c.1913,
oil on canvas, 100.3 x 67.3, Tate
Early in his career Mondrian (1872–1944)
painted landscapes in soft, muted colours.
This is based on his realistic sketches of
trees, but he reworked the image almost
to abstraction, reducing it to a grid,
symbolising a balance of physical and
spiritual forces.

© 2009 Mondrian/Holtzman Trust c/o
HCR International Warrenton VA USA

Wassily Kandinsky, *Swinging* 1925,
oil on canvas, 70.5 x 50.2, Tate
Kandinsky (1866–1944) was one of the
first to stop representing the visible
world and to paint less realistic subjects,
often linking his paintings to the flow
and rhythm of music. He believed that
art, like music, should be about emotions,
and made colour and shape as important
as any subject. The title of this painting
conveys a sense of dynamic movement.

It's hard to imagine how much the technical revolution affected people at the end of the 19th century, as rapid advances in technology are now so common. But in the 1880s and 1890s new inventions including cars, electricity, engines and cameras transformed everyone's lives.

HOW TO LOOK AT MODERN ART

There are ways to understand modern art. Begin with a few questions:

- What is it made with? Has the artist used conventional or unexpected materials? Is there a reason for this?
- What is its subject? Does the title give you a clue? An ambiguous title means that the artist was exploring an idea rather than a particular scene or subject.
- When was it made? If you know that, you can probably work out if it belonged to a particular movement or if it was commenting on something happening at the time.
- Who made it? Background knowledge of the artist helps you to understand the reasoning behind the work.
- How was it made? Was it for a particular purpose or occasion? Did the artist plan the work or leave much to chance? You might be able to find this out online or at a gallery.
- Do you like it? (You don't have to like art to appreciate it!) Look for colour, texture, elements and ideas behind the work. You might not like the way it looks, but you might be interested in the thoughts behind it.
- There is never just one interpretation of a work of art. Look carefully and think about what you see; your own response is as valid as anyone's. Try to view it with an open mind.

Photography

The invention of photography in 1839 affected artists' practice the most. Almost immediately the public wanted photographs, not paintings. Some artists questioned the need for copying the world around them when photographs could do the job with so little effort. Some artists became photographers, others tried to paint even more realistically and some used photographs to help them arrange compositions in ways that had not been considered before.

New beginnings

From the start, modern art (also sometimes called Modernism) was misunderstood and criticised while it was being produced. Some works received critical acclaim, but disapproval was the most common reaction, whereas previously art had often been respected and admired. Much of the work that was being produced could only be appreciated by other artists or was only understood when the artist explained what it meant.

Art historians disagree about when modern art began. Some link it to the French Revolution of 1789. Others say it was 1863, when an exhibition of 'modern' art was held in Paris. Whenever it was, all modern artists have believed that art should reflect their world. For years people had believed that for art to be good it had to be beautiful. That meant that art was valued purely for its appearance and not for its purpose or meaning. Gradually, the whole notion of creating art changed. It was no longer simply a case of reproducing the outward appearance of things or trying to create beauty.

WHAT CHANGED?

'Every change is a form of liberation.
My mother used to say a change is always good
even if it's for the worse.'
Paula Rego

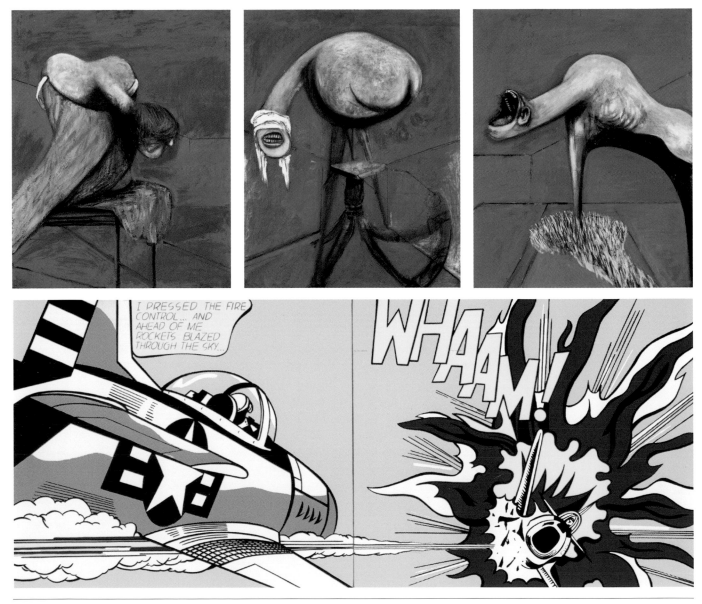

Top Francis Bacon, *Three Studies for Figures at the Base of a Crucifixion* c.1944, oil on board, 94 x 73.7, Tate
The title helps to explain the tormented facial expressions of these twisted creatures, but there is no actual crucifixion. Like many artists during the Second World War, Bacon (1909–92) found it difficult to believe in the existence of a caring God. Distortion conveys extreme emotion and red suggests fierce heat – perhaps the fires of hell. Bacon wanted viewers to share his abhorrence of war.

Bottom Roy Lichtenstein, *WHAAM!* 1963, acrylic on canvas, 172.7 x 406.4, Tate
In the USA in the 1960s Lichtenstein (1923–97) began producing massive comic-style pictures, meticulously painting thousands of giant dots across the canvas. The paintings demonstrate that comic-strip art is not as simple as it looks, with dramatic compositions and bold colours. Lichtenstein said, 'One of the things a cartoon does is to express violent emotion in a completely mechanical and removed style'.

At the turn of the 20th century, many young artists welcomed the new age with hope and anticipation. They believed that they were witnessing the beginning of an exciting new world that would be different from anything seen before. They wanted to reflect this in their work. Some began expressing a whole host of aims and ideas, using diverse materials, breaking accepted rules of art. Everyone concerned knew what these rules were and there was a lot of snobbery involved. Several artists found themselves in the middle of legal disputes about their work. It soon became difficult to understand what art was, what 'good' art was – and what wasn't art at all.

A new career

As fewer patrons commissioned work, a new career emerged: that of the art dealer. Dealers bought art from artists and sold it on, earning a percentage each time. They placed art in commercial galleries, which opened in various European cities from the mid-19th century. Before this, people mostly bought art directly from artists or at exhibitions and auctions. Now they could browse in galleries to choose what they wanted. From the start, dealers marketed art as desirable and often displayed unconventional work. Whereas before patrons had been in control over what artists produced, now artists could paint what they wanted and sell their work independently through dealers.

Rubbishing art

As some artists began challenging conventions, many people became annoyed and confused. In 1878 James McNeill Whistler (1834–1903) sued the critic John Ruskin (1819–1900) for libel after Ruskin accused Whistler of 'flinging a pot of paint in the public's face' with his painting *Nocturne in Black and Gold: the Falling Rocket*. Almost fifty years later the sculptor Constantin Brancusi (1876–1957) won a lawsuit against the US customs authorities who called his sculpture 'raw metal'. And in 2004, a cleaner threw away a bag of rubbish at Tate Britain which was actually part of Gustav Metzger's installation. Metzger (born 1926) had invented 'Auto-destructive Art' in the 1960s, which arose from his experiences of Nazi Germany and was part of his protests about politics and capitalism.

DIFFERENT ANGLES

When you think about it, paintings that try to pretend they are three-dimensional images are not telling the truth. Perspective is an illusion invented by artists in the 15th century to show us the world from one viewpoint. Paul Cézanne (1839–1906) admired past artists, but he wanted to be more honest about what he saw. So he painted pictures showing objects from several different angles at once – something photographs can't do – closer to the way we really see things.

BREAKING RULES

'One reassuring thing about modern art is that things can't be as bad as they are painted.'
Leo Tolstoy

Opposite **Fernand Léger,** *Still Life with a Beer Mug* **1921–2, oil on canvas, 107.4 x 74.7, Tate**
Léger (1881–1955) was part of a group of artists working in Paris at the beginning of the 20th century. He was influenced by Cézanne and fascinated with modern technology. His paintings combine simplified tubular forms seen from several viewpoints, as he wanted his art to reflect the world around him. His experiences fighting in the First World War made him want to make his art accessible to everyone. In the centre of this painting is a large beer mug surrounded by plates of fruit, pots of butter and a corkscrew. To the side is a blue curtain. The table's long, thin legs stand on a black and white chequered floor. This mixture of viewpoints and fascination with machines means that Léger is often linked with both Cubism and Futurism.

Paul Cézanne, *Still Life with Basket of Apples* **1890–94, oil on canvas, 65 x 80, The Art Institute of Chicago**
Cézanne was particularly interested in solid shapes and negative space. Negative space describes the shapes and spaces around and between objects. He painted objects from different viewpoints, applying gleaming colours in thick brushstrokes. The shifting perspective resembles how we really see things. This profoundly influenced 20th-century art. Picasso developed Cézanne's shapes into Cubism, and Matisse admired his use of colour. Picasso said: 'Cézanne was like the father of us all'. From then on, Cézanne was nicknamed the 'father of modern art'.

So how did (and do) artists decide what to paint or sculpt? Not all of them had life-changing experiences such as fighting for their countries. Most modern art ideas are not spontaneous. Mostly, the end results emerge gradually, and the works that we see are not always artists' complete solutions, but part of their creative journey.

ART IN CONTEXT

CRITICAL THINKING

People have strong opinions about what art should – and shouldn't – be. What do you think? Consider both opinions and facts:

- If someone has a strong viewpoint, try to decide whether that person is subjective or objective – and if so, why?
- If you hear or read about art, is the information reliable?
- Have facts been accepted too readily? It's important to find out as much information as you can about art that interests you.
- Try to be sure what is opinion and what are provable facts. Opinions are valid, but it is important to know the difference between fact and opinion.

INSPIRATION

'What moves men of genius, or rather what inspires their work, is not new ideas, but their obsession with the idea that what has already been said is still not enough.'
Eugène Delacroix

Avant-garde

Some artists, like Cézanne for instance, inspire other artists. Many original and influential artists spend their whole lives ignored or ridiculed by the art world. Then others come along and push their ideas further, and voilà! A new art style is founded. Pablo Picasso (1881–1973), for example, directly influenced by Cézanne, painted still-life objects from several angles on one flat canvas. This is how he and Georges Braque (1882–1963) developed Cubism (see pp.28–9). Artists who start movements are described as 'avant-garde', which means they initiate new approaches. The term avant-garde is applied to a number of artists, artistic styles and movements, such as Cubism, Expressionism, Futurism, Suprematism, Constructivism and Surrealism. Some common ideas cross the boundaries of several movements, and artists often work in varied ways, so 'belong' to different movements.

Great debate

Over the late 19th century and throughout the 20th century, debates raged about whether art should be self-sufficient – that is, whether it should stand alone in its own right or whether it should always be about something else. This is where the phrase 'art for art's sake' came from. Théophile Gautier (1811–72), a poet, dramatist, novelist, journalist and literary critic, introduced the idea, saying that art is valuable by itself and does not need any additional reason for its existence. The poet and art critic Charles Baudelaire (1821–67) believed that art should stand alone and not have a specific social function. The artist James McNeill Whistler declared that art should be independent and should appeal to the senses without being confused with other emotions such as pity or love. Contrastingly, the Russian novelist Leo Tolstoy (1828–1910) argued that art should not be simply attractive to look at, but it should express moral values.

Opposite Georges Braque, *Bottle and Fishes* **c.1910–12, oil on canvas, 61.9 x 74.9, Tate**
A bottle and fish on a plate are laid on a table with a drawer. Braque has purposefully splintered the shapes of the objects like broken glass to create a network of surfaces shown at different angles. He has used a limited palette of colours to focus on shapes and forms, but this makes it tricky to work out what is background and what are the objects themselves.

Piet Mondrian, *Composition C (No.III) with Red, Yellow and Blue* **1935, oil on canvas, 56 x 55.2, Tate**
Mondrian was one of the first artists to dispense with picture frames, wanting his work to be part of the world and not isolated from it. Like several other contemporary artists, Mondrian was fascinated by Theosophy – a philosophy based on spirituality. His paintings reduce everything to simple, pure colours, shapes and lines. He believed that most people were out of harmony with nature and he wanted to create a sense of peace. Here, the vertical and horizontal lines create a sense of energy and rhythm. Both Mondrian and Wassily Kandinsky believed that art should help provide people with a spiritual element which was being lost in the often violent and materialistic modern world.

So when did things change? When did people stop being horrified by art that didn't conform? Even art that appears to us to be conventional now scandalised some people when it was first shown, and often artists continue to shock and outrage, so the artistic revolution persists. Still, most people know that van Gogh was terribly poor and that Picasso was terribly rich. (Which isn't so terrible.) This means that at some point between van Gogh's death (1890) and Picasso becoming wealthy (around 1918), a number of people began understanding, and even perhaps enjoying, modern art.

ART IN CONTEXT

OTHER CULTURES

If modern art is all about newness, then why have so many artists been influenced by often primitive art from other cultures and eras? Here are some things to think about:

- As the 20th century continued, religious observance declined and fewer Westerners went to church.
- Some artists wanted to fill a 'spiritual gap' in people's lives through their art.
- Much of the art of earlier cultures focused on spiritual needs without confusing that with social codes of behaviour.
- Primitive art was seen as unchanging, mysterious and simple – values many artists felt were vanishing in the West.

THE ARTISTIC REVOLUTION

'The day is coming when a single carrot, freshly observed, will set off a revolution.'
Paul Cézanne

Attacking beliefs

Some artistic revolutions have been started by single artists, but unless others appreciate the artist's ideas, those ideas fail and that particular artist is not a revolutionary. Some artists have produced what appears to be wild and wacky work, only for society to catch up and get the message later. Like Shakespeare's fools, the best artists comment on things that are not always apparent to everyone, but which surface afterwards. In the 1870s, the Impressionists outraged the art world with their dabs of pure colour and speedy painting methods. Their work was rejected by all the official exhibitions, and even their name started as an insult. By the 1880s their stylistic revolution was popular, as people understood what they were trying to do. In the mid-1940s the first Abstract Expressionists were sharply criticised and ridiculed when they relied on their feelings to create images, but when the harsh reality of atomic bombs hit the world, their chaotic, emotional work did not seem so crazy.

Even if art is produced just for its own sake (see p.12), it still reflects contemporary society: most 'good' art comments on the society in which it is made, often pointing out right and wrong. So as times change, art, like the culture surrounding it, changes too. The best artists anticipate society's changes and show them in an unfamiliar way. Sharp perception is all part of the modern artist's skill.

Opposite Claude Monet, *Poplars on the Epte* **1891, oil on canvas, 92.4 x 73.7, Tate**
When Monet (1840–1926) learned that some poplar trees on a nearby river were to be cut down, he paid for them to be left standing for a while. He painted 23 versions of them from his boat, at different times of day and in different weather conditions. He was investigating the effects of different qualities of light. His paintings captured what we might see in a fleeting glimpse – something that photography could not do at the time. Although these paintings were a great success and most sold quickly, some critics were unsure about his approach.

Pablo Picasso, *Seated Woman in a Chemise* **1923, oil on canvas, 92.1 x 73, Tate**
Losing confidence in Western society, many artists searched for something untouched by war or materialism that might refresh art. The art of primitive cultures seemed to have all the necessary credentials. From 1907 Picasso showed the influence of art of other cultures in many of his works. This woman's features, dress and poise resemble ancient Greek statues, while the bulkiness of her limbs echo even earlier art. Picasso could paint extremely realistically, but he realised that lifelike images are just that and nothing more, so he constantly tried out new ideas.

Before 1900 artists had begun experimenting with colour in ways that hadn't been possible before, as new chemical pigments were invented and the innovation of keeping paint in tin tubes kept these colours bright and fresh. Some artists also attempted to convey feelings or symbolic meanings through colour. Some artists of the 20th and 21st centuries have portrayed modern life using unnatural colours, while others have explored the way our eyes perceive different colour combinations. Certain artists have used coloured light to change the way we view things, and at least one artist has invented his own colour!

COLOUR CONTRASTS

There are three main types of colour: primary, secondary and tertiary. Primary colours are red, yellow and blue, and can't be made from other colours. Different combinations of primary colours will create all other colours. Secondary colours are a mix of two primaries, making green, violet and orange and tertiary are a mix of primary and secondary colours. Complementary colours are colours that are opposites on the colour wheel and harmonising colours are next to each other. When placed side by side, complementaries make each other appear brighter. This is called the *law of simultaneous contrast*. Warm colours, such as reds and oranges, appear to advance or come forward, while cool colours, such as blues and greens, appear to recede or sink back.

COLOUR

'The music of colour, that's what I want.'
Bridget Riley

Dull and bright

In the past only natural pigments and dyes were available. Some were strong, while others were less intense and had to be mixed to make a desired colour. For instance, there were some clear reds and a blue, but yellows were brownish. Green was made by mixing strong blue and weak yellow, so in old paintings greens often look dull. Once chemists discovered how to make new colours, all this changed.

In 1905, when Henri Matisse (1869–1954), André Derain (1880–1954) and friends exhibited at the Autumn Salon in Paris, they caused an outrage. Their flamboyantly coloured, freely handled work was shocking (see pp.22–5). Rather than presenting reality, their colours were personal to them and were rarely dark or dull. For Matisse, intense, strong colours reflected happiness.

Experiments

During the 20th century many artists began producing images that were not of recognisable things, but were made up of distorted colours, lines and shapes. Kandinsky was one of the earliest pioneers of this abstract art (see pp.34–5): he had seen one of his paintings on its side and thought it looked more interesting that way. There are varying degrees of abstraction. Some works are completely abstract, with no links to the visible world, while others have connections although they might not look realistic. Kandinsky named some of his works after music, as he said that music affects our feelings and doesn't rely on ideas from the real world to be effective. He used colours just as musicians use notes: for instance, blue for tranquil low notes and yellow for uplifting high notes. This linked with his beliefs about the spiritual powers of colour.

Opposite Robert Delaunay, *Windows Open Simultaneously* 1912, oil on canvas, 45.7 x 37.5, Tate
The Eiffel Tower was a great technological accomplishment. This is one of thirteen paintings on this theme that Delaunay (1885–1941) painted between 1912 and 1913, based on a postcard of the Eiffel Tower. Concerned with the emotional effects of colour contrasts, he painted the energy of city life and the modern world from multiple viewpoints. The colours are arranged rhythmically across the picture's surface, suggesting a link with music.

Wassily Kandinsky, *Cossacks* 1910–11, oil on canvas, 94.6 x 130.2, Tate
This painting was also named *Battle*. Can you see anything of the real world, apart from the rainbow, here? Look closely! The three red shapes on the right are Cossack hats; the long black lines they are holding are lances, and one leans on his sabre. Behind, coming over the blue hill, are more lances, indicating more Cossacks advancing. At the top, two Cossacks fight on horseback, and above right, birds fly over a black-outlined fort. Lines, colours, gunfire and the rainbow create a disturbing contrast. This is an 'abstraction': it represents the real world in an abstract way.

As the focus moved away from making things look lifelike and towards exploring spiritual or emotional ideas, certain artists began looking at patterns and shapes.

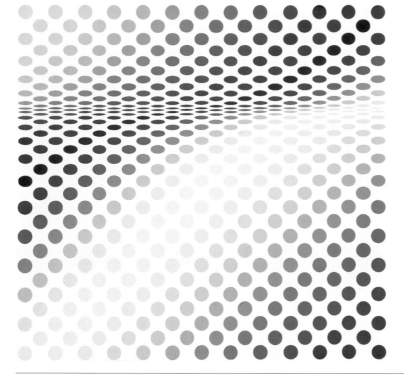

PATTERN & SHAPE

'The object of art is to give life a shape.'
William Shakespeare

Spiritual harmony and optical impressions

Like colour, shapes and patterns can describe emotion too. Scratchy, sharp shapes can be uncomfortable or unsettling, while flowing, smooth shapes can seem calm or happy. When a strong shape is put next to a smaller shape it can appear to dominate, which can create the appearance of depth. Several modern artists have made the most of the way we unconsciously respond to different shapes, including, for instance, Mondrian, Bridget Riley (born 1931) and Chris Ofili (born 1968). Neo-Plasticism (new plastic art) was a Dutch abstract movement founded by Mondrian and Theo van Doesburg (1883–1931) in 1917; they were joined by others with the same views. Neo-Plasticism removed any hint of realism from art by using only straight lines and primary colours plus black, white and grey. The resulting grid-like patterns are intended to convey tranquillity and spiritual harmony.

Since the 1960s Bridget Riley has produced strong patterns to create optical effects that generate sensations of movement, light and colour. She aims to combine these visual sensations with emotion.

Ofili is probably best known for using elephant dung in his work. Like van Gogh's earlobe, this story has been blown out of proportion. Elephant dung is used in certain rituals in Africa, which is where Ofili has his roots. He mixes a wide range of other references too, from the Bible to pornographic magazines, from 1970s comics to the work of artists such as William Blake (1757–1827). His work is usually built up in layers of paint, resin, glitter, dung and other materials. The themes and approach are frequently controversial, often referring to spiritual subjects; the swirling, colourful patterns are intended to uplift the emotions (see p.107).

Bridget Riley, *Hesitate* 1964, oil on canvas, 106.7 x 112.4, Tate
This was one of many works that became called Op art. The name referred to the optical effects that Riley creates. The curves, shapes and patterns affect us physically, making us think the painting is moving or is coloured when it isn't. This type of art is a real way of involving viewers – your eyes complete the effect.

Clean lines

Exaggerating or reducing shapes to create fresh ways of looking at the world have been investigated by many artists, such as Brancusi, whose early influences included African and oriental art, and Auguste Rodin (1840–1917). From 1907 Brancusi simplified his sculpture, aiming to create pure forms. Using the natural world as the starting point, he modelled clean lines and simple shapes, creating abstractions of real things. By simplifying and exaggerating forms, he reduced his subjects to their essential elements, creating strong patterns and streamlined effects.

Wayne Thiebaud (born 1920) is an American painter whose most famous works are of cakes, pastries, toys and lipsticks, which he has simplified to create pattern-like compositions across each canvas. Applying heavy pigment and exaggerated colours he focuses on his subjects' basic shapes, isolating triangles, circles and squares.

ILLUSIONS

One of the dominant aspects of modern life has been the rapid development of science and technology. Some artists have built on these developments in a positive way. Some, such as the Futurists and the Vorticists (see pp.38–41) and the Op artists (see pp.84–5) have tried to capture the dynamism of the machine age, using patterns and shapes to create illusions that make their motionless art appear to move.

Constantin Brancusi, *Danaïde* c.1918, bronze on limestone base, 27.9 x 17, Tate
This is a Hungarian art student called Margit Pogany, whom Brancusi met in Paris in 1910. Brancusi made the head from memory, then invited her to his studio and she was delighted to recognise herself. He had refined her facial features to their purest, simplest and most descriptive forms. It is clear that she had a round face with large eyes and strong eyebrows, and she wore her hair pulled back in a chignon. Brancusi's work influenced the streamlined style of Art Deco in the 1920s and 1930s.

19

At the end of the 19th century and up to the start of the First World War, with many political, cultural, technological and artistic changes, a new idea called Modernism emerged. Modernists welcomed change and rejected old traditions, believing that for the new century everything, including art, architecture, religious beliefs and even daily life, should be modernised. At about the same time as Modernism, artists around the world began searching for a new art.

Art Nouveau

As a response to the sweeping changes caused by the urban growth and technological advances that followed the Industrial Revolution, a new and original movement emerged. Art Nouveau incorporated all forms of art and design, including architecture and fine art. Although artists interpreted it differently around the world, its main features were swirling, flowing designs often based on plants, flames or the female form and inspired by Japanese designs. Materials such as iron, glass, silver and pewter and soft colours were frequently used, contrasting with the heavy, ornate designs of the Victorian age.

Jewel-like

The Vienna Secession was the Austrian version of Art Nouveau. Gustav Klimt (1862–1918) was one of the leading members of the movement. His favourite subjects were women and many of his works are embellished with gold leaf and jewel-like patterns, which is understandable as his father was a goldsmith and Klimt himself trained in mosaics. He visited Venice and Ravenna, both famous for their golden Byzantine mosaics, and was also influenced by Egyptian, Minoan and Classical Greek art, as well as the engravings of Albrecht Dürer (1471–1528). Combining both fine and decorative arts, he became successful, yet for years his nudes were considered rude and shocking. Ahead of his time, his work also investigated the power that women have over men.

Flowing lines

Klimt taught Egon Schiele (1890–1918), and influenced him hugely. Schiele mainly painted figures, and often young women, barely dressed, in distorted poses and mottled colours. His figures look out at the viewer boldly. At a time when women were still wearing long skirts, many found the sexual obviousness of Schiele's works disturbing. In 1912 he was arrested for having pornographic drawings in his studio. After a short time in prison he returned to his expressive paintings then in 1915 he was called up to fight in the First World War. He spent most of his time in the army painting and by 1917, on his return to Austria, the outrage he had caused had lessened and he became the leading Austrian artist of the younger generation – but only for a short time, as he contracted Spanish flu and died at the age of just 28.

KLIMT & SCHIELE

'The aim of art is to represent not the outward appearance of things, but their inward significance.'
Aristotle

Gustav Klimt, *Portrait of Hermine Gallia*
1904, oil on canvas, 170.5 x 96.5, Tate
Hermine's husband, Moritz Gallia,
was a leading patron of the arts.
He commissioned Klimt, the most
controversial artist of the day, to paint
his wife. Klimt designed her dress and
produced many drawings. He made
several alterations to the final painting:
for instance, he reshaped the contours
of the dress. Klimt shows Hermine as a
relaxed, modern woman, even though
the pose, dress and setting were highly
unconventional for a formal portrait at
the time.

Egon Schiele, *Reclining Woman With*
Black Stockings **1917, gouache and black**
crayon, 29.4 x 46, Private collection
Schiele moved away completely from the
expected demure poses and expressions
of portraits in the previous century,
and seemed determined to expose
uncomfortable feelings through his art.
Unusually for the time, this young
woman has messy hair and stares directly
at us. Although she looks confident, there
is also something fragile and gloomy
about her.

Back at the end of the 19th century (again), artists such as Georges Seurat (1859–91), Paul Gauguin (1848–1903), Paul Signac (1863–1935) and Vincent van Gogh (1853–90) found new ways of representing nature. They used different colours and marks to paint pictures that represented more than just a copy of things around us.

LOOKING FOR CLUES

In a lifelike painting or sculpture, emotion is shown mainly through people's poses or expressions, but in unrealistic works, how do we identify the point the artist is making? Consider some of these ideas:

- Can you recognise any expression? Faces can be portrayed with simple lines and sometimes even basic marks can describe a look of anger, horror or happiness, for instance.
- What are the predominant shapes? Swirls can imply happiness or turmoil; jagged shapes can mean anger or pain; angles can mean conflict, while smooth shapes can signify harmony.
- Are the colours calm or violent? How are they applied? Thick paint can show anger or pleasure, it all depends on whether the brushstrokes are long or short.

By responding to these visual clues instinctively (without thinking too much) we can usually sense the mood or message of most works.

FAUVISM

'Great art picks up where nature ends.'
Marc Chagall

Can you see their point?
Seurat invented a technique known as 'pointillism' (he called it 'divisionism'), creating pictures with small dots of pure colour. Seen from a distance, the dots blend together, making new colours. Signac was also a pointillist, but his dots were slightly bigger and more mosaic-like. As president of the annual Salon des Indépendants (an official art exhibition that had been held in Paris since 1884), from 1908 until his death, Signac encouraged younger artists (he was the first to buy a painting by Matisse) and exhibited controversial works.

As if dots and squares weren't enough, in Paris in 1905, at the Salon d'Automne, some artists exhibited paintings with vivid, flattened colours and warped images. People were horrified and a critic nicknamed them 'Les Fauves', which means 'wild beasts'. Matisse and Derain were among the artists. Many of the Fauve characteristics first appeared in Matisse's work during the summer of 1904 whilst he was in Saint-Tropez with Signac. Matisse became the leader of the group, but other members were just as notorious. They included Maurice de Vlaminck (1876–1958), Raoul Dufy (1877–1953), Braque (who later developed Cubism with Picasso), Albert Marquet (1875–1947) and Georges Rouault (1871–1958). Although they had an assortment of styles, they all experimented with colour-drenched canvases applied with stubby brushstrokes. They were not trying to pretend that their pictures were part of real life – skin could be painted blue or green, grass and sky could be red – it all depended on what emotions they were conveying and nothing had to look three-dimensional at all!

Opposite **André Derain, *Henri Matisse*
1905, oil on canvas, 46 x 34.9, Tate**
Derain and Matisse studied together
in Paris in 1898. Encouraged by Matisse,
in 1904 Derain began using strong,
unnatural colours, applied in small
brushstrokes to convey sensations of
light and shade. During a holiday in the
South of France in 1905, they painted
portraits of each other. Derain has used
the 'wrong' colours deliberately: blue
shadows contrast with complementary
orange highlights (see p.16). What other
colours have been put together
deliberately?

Top **André Derain, *The Pool of London*
1906, oil on canvas, 65.7 x 99.1, Tate**
This view from London Bridge shows the
River Thames with Tower Bridge in the
distance. Derain had been sent to London
by his dealer to paint some popular
Thames views that had been painted by
Monet a few years earlier. The painting
is typical of Fauvism with its distorted
shapes and vivid colour contrasts.

Bottom **Maurice de Vlaminck, *Landscape
near Martigues* 1913, oil on canvas,
65.1 x 81.9, Tate**
Vlaminck often applied paint straight
from the tube, without using a brush, in
order to keep the colour bright. When he
did use brushes, his brushstrokes were
broad and thick. This landscape appears
flat, as it is meant to look like a painting –
a characteristic of the Fauves. The patches
of colour create liveliness and a sense of
movement.

Matisse became one of the most influential and best-known artists of the 20th century. He was unusual in that his work was always all about happiness, unlike a lot of modern artists whose works revolve around their depression or anger.

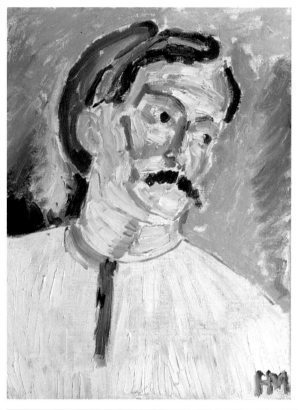

MATISSE

'A picture must possess a real power to generate light and for a long time now I've been conscious of expressing myself through light or rather in light.'
Henri Matisse

Brighter than nature
In 1887 Matisse's father sent him to study law in Paris. He completed his certificate in a year. Then in 1890, recovering from appendicitis, his mother gave him a box of paints. That was it. Sixty years later he remembered: 'It was as if I had been called. Henceforth, I did not lead my life. It led me.'

In 1896 Matisse visited the artist John Peter Russell (1858–1930), who was an Impressionist painter and had been a friend of van Gogh's. Never having seen an Impressionist painting, Matisse was so shocked at the style that he left after ten days, saying that he 'couldn't stand it'. The following year he returned as Russell's student and abandoned his earth-coloured palette for bright colours. From then on all his paintings were vibrantly coloured: he painted colours brighter than nature, even though they were called barbaric when he first exhibited them in 1905. He said: 'I don't paint things. I only paint the difference between things.'

Influences
As a student of Odilon Redon (1840–1916), Matisse had closely studied the work of Edouard Manet (1832–83) and Cézanne. Then in 1904 he became interested in Seurat's pointillism. Seurat was long dead by this time, but Matisse became friends with his follower Paul Signac, who had great influence on his work, and in 1905 he went south again to work with Derain. At this point his colour exploded, and from then on he only produced images that promoted happiness or calmness. He once said that he wanted his art to have the effect of a good armchair on a tired businessman.

Pattern and space
Matisse loved pattern: those he invented, and also oriental carpets, tapestries and embroideries, all of which added to the cheerfulness of his work. As well as his beautiful colours, his balanced eye and his fluid and original draughtsmanship, he was also a printmaker and sculptor. In his work, what he left out is just as important as what he included, and his use of space makes nearly everything he produced fresh and filled with light.

Henri Matisse, *André Derain* 1905, oil on canvas, 39.4 x 28.9, Tate
This is the portrait that Matisse painted of Derain while Derain painted him (see p.22) when they were in the South of France. Using glowing colours Matisse captured the sensation of sunlight on Derain's face that cast a heavy shadow down one side. The complementary colours, including blue and orange, red and green, make the picture strong – Matisse's use of colour was revolutionary.

Henri Matisse, *The Snail* 1953, gouache on paper, cut and pasted on paper mounted on canvas, 286.4 x 287, Tate

This work is huge. At first glance it looks like a random arrangement of brightly coloured shapes on a white background, but on closer inspection the shapes are in a loose spiral suggesting the shape of a snail's shell. Instead of being painted directly onto canvas, the shapes are made from big pieces of paper that have been painted in a water-based paint called gouache. Then these were torn and cut into shapes and stuck onto a white paper background. Finally, the whole composition was glued onto canvas. This is one of the last and largest pieces in Matisse's final series of works, known as 'cut-outs'. Aged 84, he was ill in bed so he instructed assistants to paint the paper, which he then tore and cut. The spiralling arrangement is extremely well balanced with complementary colour placed next to each other. Matisse believed that he had reduced shapes and colours to their essentials. He had two little jokes going here – one was the size and colour of the work in comparison to a real, tiny, brown snail, and the other was the tiny cut-out shape of the snail at the top of the lilac shape. They don't tell 'em like that anymore.

Many of Rodin's sculptures were criticised during his lifetime because they were not traditional. Unlike the perfect figures of Ancient Greece, he modelled the human body with lifelike frankness. Although sensitive to criticism, Rodin didn't change his style and gradually his reputation grew. By 1900, he was world-renowned. His 'warts-and-all' approach caused problems when one of his early works looked so realistic that he was accused of having taken a cast from a living model, although he was eventually cleared. Over more than fifty years, he produced thousands of sculptures, drawings and paintings. Fascinated by dance and spontaneous movement, he worked with street performers, acrobats and dancers, rather than using professional models. Many of his sculptures appear unfinished, hewn out of rough lumps of rock. This was to encourage viewers to use their imaginations.

Pure forms

As a newcomer to Paris, Brancusi (see p.10), a Romanian sculptor who trained originally as a carpenter and stonemason, was fascinated by Rodin's work. Although he went on to work in a different style altogether, Rodin was his first and most influential teacher. Brancusi also admired primitive art. After leaving Rodin's workshop he began developing his revolutionary style. He aimed to depict 'not the outer form but the idea, the essence of things', believing that extra details were superfluous to creating a pure work of art. The only way to create something pure was to carve into a hunk of stone, metal, wood or limestone. This method mixed simplicity and sophistication that led the way for Modernist sculptors. Brancusi's work inspired many other sculptors, including Barbara Hepworth (1903–75), Carl Andre (born 1935) and Donald Judd (1928–94).

Spindly figures

Just as Brancusi didn't think we all have egg-shaped heads, so Alberto Giacometti (1901–66) didn't think a) we are all block-heads or b) that we should all lose several pounds in weight. A Swiss sculptor working in Paris, Giacometti was involved with the Surrealists (see pp.66–7). His early works involved taking the natural shapes of large stones and doing little to them to make them resemble something figurative – a bit like converting a doodle into a picture. He went on to make Surrealist constructions out of metal, wood and other materials. Talking of doodles, his drawings are fascinatingly fluid, made up of scribbled lines that show planes and structure in detail. His spindly, elongated metal figures caught the imagination of the public, seen as reflecting the absurdity of life in war-damaged Europe.

RODIN, BRANCUSI & GIACOMETTI

'The people who call my work "abstract" are imbeciles … what they call "abstract" is in fact the purest realism, the reality of which is not represented by external form but by the idea behind it, the essence of the work.'
Constantin Brancusi

Auguste Rodin, *The Kiss* 1901–4, pentelican marble, 182.2 x 121.9 x 153, Tate
Rodin produced three life-sized, lifelike versions of these two kissing. They are Francesca da Rimini and her husband's brother Paolo Malatesta. They fell in love reading the story of Lancelot and Guinevere together (can you spot the book?) Then Francesca's husband came in and, not too happy, killed them both. Dante wrote about them in his Divine Comedy. When Rodin created the first version, the Columbian Exposition in Chicago rejected it for being too erotic for public display.

TAKING IT APART

When you look at a work of modern sculpture, the following questions might help you to understand it:

- Should sculpture copy the real world? Copying real life is skilful when done well, but isn't it more interesting to see other ideas as well?
- Why have so many artists focused on imagination, emotion and purity? If you were a sculptor, what would you focus on?
- What is sculpture for? What is its place in society?
- Why has the human figure continued to be such an important subject?
- Does the title help you to understand the work? Does the setting? (Where is the work?)
- How important is the material it is made from? Would it be as effective in another material?

Alberto Giacometti, *Man Pointing* 1947, bronze, 178 x 95 x 52, Tate
More worried about what he was trying to do than what others thought of his work, Giacometti often reworked his sculpture over long periods before casting them in bronze, building up the clay model, then stripping it down, rebuilding and stripping again, as he gradually eroded the outline of the body to its essential core.

Constantin Brancusi, *Maiastra* 1911, bronze and stone, 90.5 x 17.1 x 17.8, Tate
This polished golden bird featured in Romanian folk tales as having miraculous powers. Brancusi was creating an idealised version of nature.

Braque and Picasso really shaped Cubism. (Literally.) Cézanne had started the idea when he said: 'Treat nature as cylinders, spheres and cones.' Braque and Picasso took it even further. They wanted to discover a method of representation that went beyond the conventional ways of conveying space. They weren't trying to imitate real life or pretend that flat canvases had depth. They believed that showing only one view of an object didn't explain it well enough, so they included several views at once. Braque explained that the goal of Cubist art was in the reality of the mind, not of sight. They didn't try to copy form, texture, colour and space; instead, they painted parts of objects, showing several angles simultaneously.

Other Cubist artists included Léger, Juan Gris (1887–1927), Marcel Duchamp (1887–1968), Jean Metzinger (1883–1956) and Francis Picabia (1879–1953). Though primarily associated with painting, Cubism also had a profound influence on 20th-century sculpture and architecture and it had far-reaching consequences for other art movements, including Dada and Surrealism.

Different phases
Using techniques and materials that were not usually used in fine art, Cubism went through two different stages between about 1907 and 1914 when the First World War brought almost everything – including artistic activity – to an abrupt end. But even after the War, Cubism was a major influence on art. By breaking up what we see, painting subjects from a variety of angles and showing different aspects altogether, Cubists really were showing three dimensions in two dimensions. Up to 1912 this was known as Analytical Cubism, when the artists concentrated on geometrical forms and used subdued colours. The second phase, known as Synthetic Cubism (from 1913 onwards), used more decorative shapes, stencilling, collage (including cut-up newspaper) and brighter colours. The style incorporated outside influences, such as African art, as well as new theories on the nature of reality, such as Einstein's Theory of Relativity, and was seen as a revolutionary way of representing the world.

Abstraction
Braque and Picasso did not begin with the idea that they were inventing a new and important art form. Their experiments were done mainly for themselves and a few wealthy people who bought their paintings, and neither of them exhibited their Cubist work publicly. The name Cubism was an insult, made up by a critic; the artists didn't mind the nickname, though, as it got them noticed. As they fragmented their images even more, their paintings became increasingly abstract and difficult to understand, so in order to give clues about what was going on they incorporated words and then 'real things'. This was the start of the idea that you can use real objects directly in art. It also opened up lots of possibilities for the treatment of reality in art.

Up to 1910 the subject of a picture was usually detectable, but after that it was often confusing. Objects and figures were reduced to overlapping planes and shapes mostly in browns, greys, or blacks, depicting little of the recognisable world.

CUBISM

'If my husband ever met a woman on the street who looked like one of his paintings he would faint.'
Jacqueline Roque (wife of Pablo Picasso)

**Juan Gris, *Bottle of Rum and Newspaper*
1913–14, oil on canvas, 46 x 37, Tate**
Bars and cafés were popular meeting
places for artists in Paris and often
featured in their work. The bottle and
newspaper in this scene are shown with
a few clues, while the mock wood grain
suggests a table top. Gris commented:
'The man who, when he paints a bottle,
attempts to express its material
substance rather than paint a group
of coloured forms, should become a glass-
blower not a painter'.

**Pablo Picasso, *Bowl of Fruit, Violin and
Bottle* 1914, oil on canvas, 92 x 73, Tate**
This is the top of a table; the fruit bowl,
violin, bottle and newspaper are all made
from areas of colour that look like cut-out
pieces of paper. Picasso and Braque had
been making collages that experimented
with representation and reality since
1912. They soon began to suggest the
appearance of collage materials in their
oil paintings, sometimes adding sand to
the paint to give a heightened reality to
the picture surface.

Why was the Spanish artist Pablo Ruiz y Picasso (just part of his name) so special? Well, without him, a lot of modern art would not have occurred as he challenged many accepted beliefs about art. As a young boy, his artistic talent was obvious and until he was 17, he spent hours copying the works of old masters and won prizes for his lifelike works. But because he could paint so realistically, he questioned what the point was – and set about changing things. His arrogance, brilliance and a pioneering spirit caused people to alter their definitions of art and accept new ways of looking at things.

IN HIDING

During the Second World War Picasso remained in German-occupied Paris. His artistic style did not fit the Nazi views of art, so he couldn't show his work during that time. In his studio he continued to paint, and although the Germans outlawed bronze casting in Paris, Picasso continued, using bronze smuggled in to him.

PICASSO

'All children are artists. The problem is how to remain an artist once he grows up.'
Pablo Picasso

Revolutionary ideas

After studying art in Madrid Picasso moved to Paris, and for several years he divided his time between Barcelona and Paris, building his reputation and circle of influential friends. One of his most famous paintings, *Les Demoiselles d'Avignon*, was produced in 1907, inspired by African artefacts and Cézanne. Unlike anything that had been seen before, this work is possibly the most revolutionary painting of the 20th century and it changed many attitudes towards art.

Innovative styles

Picasso's work is often categorised into periods. After the suicide of a close friend, his Blue Period, from 1901 to 1904, consists of paintings of sad-looking, thin people in shades of blue. The Rose Period of 1904 to 1906 was more optimistic, with warm pink colours and slightly happier people. The African-influenced period lasted roughly from 1907 to 1909 and Analytic Cubism continued until 1912, with Synthetic Cubism carrying on until the First World War. After 1918 he painted in a neoclassical style, influenced by the work of Jean Auguste Dominique Ingres (1780–1867); and by the 1930s one of his most famous works was his depiction of the German bombing of Guernica during the Spanish Civil War. This large canvas symbolises the brutality and hopelessness of war (see pp.74–5). Asked to explain its symbolism, Picasso said: 'It isn't up to the painter to define the symbols ... The public who look at the picture must interpret the symbols as they understand them.'

Diversity

Assorted styles and materials are a common part of Picasso's work. During the late 1940s and 1950s he produced several sculptures and other constructions using many different kinds of media, such as toys, glass, wood and ceramics.

Opposite Pablo Picasso, *Weeping Woman* 1937, oil on canvas, 60.8 x 50, Tate
One of the worst atrocities of the Spanish Civil War was the bombing of the town of Guernica by the German air force, in support of General Franco. Picasso responded to the massacre by painting the massive mural *Guernica* and made further paintings based on the horror of the atrocity. The bombing happened on a Sunday in April 1937, when the women and children were coming out of church. Ignoring traditional perspective here, Picasso depicts the scene from several angles. German fighter planes are reflected in the distressed woman's eyes as she watches innocent people being killed and maimed, the centre of her face turning to shards of ice as the true horror sinks in. Poignantly, she still wears her Sunday best hat. Her features are based on Picasso's girlfriend at the time, Dora Maar.

Pablo Picasso, *Les Demoiselles d'Avignon* 1907, oil on canvas, 243.9 x 233.7, Museum of Modern Art, New York
This work affected modern art possibly more than any other. Five prostitutes look at us. All are composed of flat, splintered planes rather than rounded shapes. Two women push aside curtains; all their eyes are lopsided and two have masks for heads. The space around them should recede, but instead it is flat and jagged. In the still life at the bottom, the fruit appears to fall off the canvas, hinting at Cézanne's ideas; the faces are influenced by African and Iberian masks. Picasso was the first modern artist to be influenced by primitive art.

31

At the beginning of the 20th century the search for ways to represent emotions expressively became a principal aim for many artists. Using new, chemically-prepared, intense colours, applying exaggerated shapes and visible brushwork, these artists expressed their emotions in differing ways. They deliberately distorted subject matter and colour to express their state of mind, or to depict sensitive issues that they thought should be addressed. This became called Expressionism. It was not a single style or movement but a subjective approach to art, and often the feelings expressed were uncomfortable and intensely personal to the artist.

NAÏVE ART

Naïve art describes a childlike style of painting. Many avant-garde artists aspired to paint in this way – indeed, Picasso said: 'It took me four years to paint like Raphael, but a lifetime to paint like a child.' Henri Rousseau (1844–1910) was a self-taught naïve artist. Many of his paintings are jungle scenes although he never left France, so he probably painted from the Parisian Botanical Gardens and from books. People ridiculed his work, saying that he didn't know what he was doing, but many modern artists, including the Expressionists, aspired to paint in his uncomplicated way.

Passionate paintings

Usually, Expressionism describes three early 20th-century art movements: Brücke (German for 'Bridge' – see below), Der Blaue Reiter (German for 'the Blue Rider' – see pp.34–5) and Les Fauves (see pp.22–3). There were also a number of artists working at the same time who are linked to Expressionism, including Oskar Kokoschka (1886–1980), Rouault, Chaim Soutine (1893–1943) and Schiele (see pp.20–1). All the artists concerned rejected the naturalism of Impressionism and were inspired by artists such as van Gogh, Gauguin, Henri de Toulouse-Lautrec (1864–1901) and Edvard Munch (1863–1944). They also admired non-European and primitive art forms. Fauvists celebrated colour and brighter emotions, while the German Expressionists frequently dwelt on darker aspects of the human mind.

Rouault trained with Matisse and exhibited with the Fauves, but his colours and subject matter are closer to the German Expressionists. He was deeply religious and used strong, rich colours in thick layers, often with black outlines, to depict desolate figures in an unrealistic but compassionate way.

A bridge to the future

In Dresden, Germany in 1905, a group of artists decided that their work would serve as a bridge to the art of the future and named themselves 'Brücke'. Frequently using intense colours, they flattened perspective and distorted shapes, and were also influenced by art from Africa and Oceania. They believed that their criticism of the ugliness of modern life could lead to a new and better future. Ernst Ludwig Kirchner (1880–1938) was the main Brücke artist. Others included Karl Schmidt-Rottluff (1884–1976), Max Pechstein (1881–1955) and Emil Nolde (1867–1956). Max Beckmann (1884–1950) rejected the movement, but is usually classified as an Expressionist because many of his paintings express the agonies of Europe at the time. By 1913, with the approach of the First World War, Brücke was dissolved.

EXPRESSIONISM

'Every production of an artist should be the expression of an adventure of his soul.'
W. Somerset Maugham

Opposite **Edvard Munch,** *The Sick Child*
1907, oil on canvas, 118.7 x 121, Tate
Munch's sister died at the age of 15. Over
20 years later he completed several
versions of this painting, exploring
haunting thoughts about his sister's
tragic death. His powerful treatment of
emotional themes was a major influence
on the development of German
Expressionism.

Top **Karl Schmidt-Rottluff,** *Two Women*
1912, oil on canvas, 76.5 x 84.5, Tate
This painting was probably inspired by
Schmidt-Rottluff's summer holidays, as
the dunes, grasslands and fishing villages
appear in several of his paintings. The
women's faces resemble masks from
Cameroon in West Africa, which many
Brücke artists saw as examples of an
unspoilt culture.

Bottom **Ernst Ludwig Kirchner,** *Bathers*
at Moritzburg 1909/26, oil on canvas,
151.1 x 199.7, Tate
Between 1909 and 1911 Kirchner and
other members of Brücke spent part of
each summer at the Moritzburg Lakes
near Dresden. The strongly contrasting
colours and distorted shapes in this
painting and others of the same theme
explored themes about nature, women
and nudity that were frowned upon in
polite society.

The Blue Rider (Der Blaue Reiter) was a German Expressionist movement lasting from 1911 until 1914. Wassily Kandinsky and Franz Marc (1880–1916) founded the group. Several other artists, including August Macke (1887–1914), Alexej von Jawlensky (1864–1941), Marianne von Werefkin (1860–1938), Lyonel Feininger (1871–1956) and Paul Klee (1879–1940) were also involved.

THE BLUE RIDER

'Colour is the keyboard, the eyes are the hammers, the soul is the piano with many strings. The artist is the hand that plays, touching one key or another purposively, to cause vibrations in the soul.'
Wassily Kandinsky

Spirituality

Kandinsky and Marc considered Cubism too calculated and wanted to revive the naïve painting of Henri Rousseau (see p.32). In 1912 they published some essays on art under the title *Almanac Der Blaue Reiter* (*Almanac of the Blue Rider*). The name was chosen probably because Marc loved horses, and his paintings of them and other animals was all part of the 'turning back to nature' approach. One of Kandinsky's paintings of 1903 is called *The Blue Rider*.

Although their approaches varied – some painted figuratively and others moved towards abstraction – each artist in the group wanted to express personal religious or social beliefs. They believed in connections between art and music, spiritual and symbolic associations of colour, and a spontaneous approach to painting. They were interested in European medieval art and primitivism, as well as some new ideas: Marc, for instance, tried to show how humans had lost their connection with nature and the environment. All the artists involved tried to investigate what was going on in people's minds and to point out that life should not be about power or materialism, but about recreating harmony in the world. But they were too late: the outbreak of the First World War in 1914 brought Der Blaue Reiter to an abrupt end, and both Marc and Macke were killed in combat. Kandinsky, von Werefkin and von Jawlensky were forced to move back to Russia. In 1923 Kandinsky, Feininger, Klee and von Jawlensky formed Die Blaue Vier (the Blue Four) and exhibited and lectured together in America.

Wassily Kandinsky

Russian born Kandinsky has been called the 'father of abstract art'. With a strong musical and artistic background, he called many of his paintings 'Compositions', 'Improvisations', 'Harmonies' or 'Impressions', which are titles usually used for music, saying that music does not have to be 'about' anything, so why should art always have to have a subject? Another reason why Kandinsky linked colour with music was due to his synaesthesia, a condition that many artistic people possess, where they either 'hear' or 'see' colours when music is played or words are spoken. Kandinsky was also extremely spiritual, which was clear first in his paintings and later in his writing about them.

Wassily Kandinsky, *Improvisation No.7 (Storm)* 1910, oil on board, 70 x 48.7, Yale University Art Gallery
Kandinsky had trained as a lawyer and he liked to think. Some might say too much. (Remember, his thoughts were full of colour). After a visit to the opera, he said: 'I saw all my colours in spirit, before my eyes. Wild, almost crazy lines were sketched in front of me.' The art critic Roger Fry called his work 'visual music'.

At the age of 30 he gave up his successful law career and moved to Germany. He travelled, mostly around Europe, between 1903 and 1908, studying art and then returning to Munich where he formed Der Blaue Reiter with Franz Marc in 1911. After the First World War, he returned to Germany and taught at the Bauhaus (see pp.58–9) until it was closed by the Nazis in 1933. He was once again forced to leave Germany, but this time moved to France.

THE COLOUR BLUE

Blue was of special importance to Kandinsky and Marc, because of its mystical significance. For Kandinsky, blue was the colour of spirituality: a book he wrote in 1911 called *On the Spiritual in Art*, discusses this. 'The power of profound meaning is found in blue. Blue is the typical heavenly colour. The ultimate feeling it creates is one of rest.' Blue has appealed to several other painters quite profoundly at times.

Franz Marc, *The Fate of the Animals*
1913, oil on canvas, 196 x 266,
Kunstmuseum, Basel
Franz Marc loved animals and, ahead of his time, was concerned with the need for harmony with nature. This huge painting, painted just before the First World War, shows the destruction of the natural world by industrialisation. Most of Marc's work portrays animals, usually in bright primary colours, with simplicity and emotion.

Although there are far too many great modern artists to fit in this book, three in particular illustrate the mood and developments of the early 20th century.

Käthe Kollwitz

Käthe Schmidt Kollwitz (1867–1945) was a German painter, printmaker and sculptor who produced expressive and powerful images of victims of poverty, hunger and war. Her art was full of compassion for the poor, the suffering and the sick, and her dark subject matter commented on social conditions in contemporary Germany. After 1891 she lived in one of the poorest parts of Berlin and her own life was marred by hardship and heartache. Her son died in the First World War and her grandson was killed in the Second World War. In 1943, her home was bombed and then, harassed by the Nazi regime she was forbidden to exhibit, as her art was classified as 'degenerate'.

Ernst Ludwig Kirchner

As one of the founders of Brücke, Kirchner was determined to inspire others with his ideas. He was a hugely enthusiastic and prolific artist. In his search for simplicity he was strongly influenced by Oceanic and African art, and he used colour to emphasise his expressive shapes. Much of his work epitomised the hectic nature of life in Berlin at the time. During the First World War he volunteered for army service, but suffered a nervous breakdown and was discharged. In 1933, still ill, his work was classed as 'degenerate' by the Nazis and he committed suicide.

DEGENERATE ART

'Degenerate art' is the English translation of the German term (entartete kunst) adopted by the Nazis to describe a great deal of modern art that didn't look like photographs. Those classed as degenerate artists faced punishments, including being dismissed from teaching positions, forbidden from exhibiting or selling their art and, in some cases, from producing art entirely. Degenerate artists were branded as enemies of the state and a threat to German culture.

KOLLWITZ, KLEE & KIRCHNER

'Art does not reproduce what we see; rather, it makes us see.'
Paul Klee

Käthe Kollwitz, *Woman with Dead Child* 1903, etching, 42.7 x 48.5, British Museum, London
This haunting etching echoes Kollwitz's concerns. A cross-legged woman hugs the body of a dead child lying limp in her arms, her grief enveloping the child. This is one of a series of works that began with a series Kollwitz called 'Pieta', of Mary mourning Christ, her dead son. These soon evolved into a series of prints and drawings of an ordinary woman with her dead child. Kollwitz's son Peter, who posed for the dead child in this etching when he was seven, was killed in the First World War 14 years later.

Paul Klee

Born in Switzerland, Klee inherited his father's German nationality. He worked with many different types of media – oil paint, watercolour, ink and more, and often mixed them. Variously called an Expressionist, Cubist and Surrealist, his work has a delicate, child-like quality and frequently suggests poetry, music and dreams, sometimes including words or musical notes. His later works contain symbols which he described as 'taking a line for a walk'. He became associated with Der Blaue Reiter along with his friend Kandinsky. Throughout his career Klee used colour in different ways, originally believing that it could only ever be just decoration. Then in 1914, when in Tunisia, he wrote: 'Colour has taken possession of me … it has hold of me forever.' Visits to Italy and Egypt also influenced him. During the First World War he painted camouflage on aeroplanes for the German army.

Klee was one of Die Blaue Vier, with Kandinsky, Feininger and von Jawlensky; they lectured and exhibited together in the USA in 1924. He also taught colour mixing and theory at the Bauhaus. In 1933 he was condemned by the Nazis for producing 'degenerate art'.

Paul Klee, *Red and White Domes* 1914, watercolour and body colour on Japanese vellum mounted on cardboard, 14.6 x 13.7, Kunstsammlung Nordrhein-Westfalen, Düsseldorf
Klee's style changed throughout his life. As the First World War began, he built up compositions of coloured squares that have the radiance of the mosaics he saw on his travels to Italy.

In 1909 some Italian artists adopted the name 'Futurism'. The Italian poet Filippo Tommaso Marinetti (1876–1944) was the first among them to publish their aims in a manifesto (a public declaration of principles and intentions). Marinetti invented and inspired the ideas behind Futurism, which included a hatred of concepts from the past, especially political and artistic traditions. The Futurists insisted on how wonderful machines were, until they entered the First World War and those very machines, in the form of guns, tanks and aeroplanes, killed so many – including some of them.

MANIFESTOS

Art manifestos were a feature of some avant-garde art movements. They usually voiced extreme opinions and were written to shock and revolutionise. They often addressed wider issues than just art, such as the political system. Manifestos expressed the ideas of the whole art group, even if only one or two people wrote the words. The first manifesto was the Futurists' in Italy in 1909 and was followed by manifestos for the Vorticists, Dadaists and the Surrealists. As other media developed, manifestos seemed less important.

Fighting talk

The extent of the Futurists' rebellion becomes clear when they are seen in the context of their heritage, of which most Italians are justifiably proud. They came from the same country as the great Renaissance artists Leonardo, Michelangelo, Raphael, Botticelli and Caravaggio, to name a few, but the Futurists rejected them. They even rejected pasta! Instead, they praised 'originality, however daring, however violent', dismissed art critics as useless and rebelled against harmony and good taste. They celebrated change and innovation, loved new technology, especially machines with their speed and power, and they believed that they loved violence and conflict. Their manifesto was aggressive and intended to attract attention and to rouse public anger and controversy.

Searching for a style

The Futurists' manifesto did not contain a definite artistic programme, but said that they should show 'universal dynamism' in painting and sculpture. They were fairly slow to develop a distinctive style and subject matter. In 1910 and 1911 some tried pointillism, applying dots and dashes inspired by Seurat (see p.22). In 1911 some adopted methods of the Cubists. Both these styles were explored, with an emphasis on the effects of speed and movement. The Futurists experimented with every medium of art, including painting, sculpture, poetry, theatre, music and architecture. They went on to publish more aggressive manifestos – in one they even demanded that galleries and museums should be pulled down – and staged events that were designed to shock.

The Futurists also celebrated city life, often painting modern urban scenes. Their first major exhibition was held in Milan in April 1911. A year later the first major exhibition of Futurist sculpture was shown in Paris. Some of the Futurists were: Carlo Carrà (1881–1966), Umberto Boccioni (1882–1916), Gino Severini (1883–1966) and Giacomo Ballà (1871–1958).

FUTURISM

'There is neither painting, nor sculpture, nor music, nor poetry. The only truth is creation.'
Umberto Boccioni

Opposite Umberto Boccioni, *Unique Forms of Continuity in Space* 1913, cast 1972, bronze, 117.5 x 87.6 x 36.8, Tate
As industrialisation swept across Italy in the early years of the 20th century; the Futurist movement enthused about speed. In this sculpture the figure is distorted by movement. Boccioni exaggerated the body's movements – muscles and clothes rippling as the person strides ahead into the future. Boccioni had developed these shapes over two years in paintings, drawings and sculptures. The result is a three-dimensional portrait of a powerful body in action.

Top Gino Severini, *Suburban Train Arriving in Paris* 1915, oil on canvas, 88.6 x 115.6, Tate

Fractured, overlapping forms zigzag across the canvas as a train arrives in Paris. This work is all about speed and machinery but also about fun. The train was loaded with weapons or soldiers, which Severini believed (in 1915), were signs of hope and excitement. Borrowing from the Cubists, the word 'KNEIPP' in the upper centre comes from a poster, advertising a malted drink, which adds to the 'modern' image he was portraying.

Bottom Giacomo Ballà, *Abstract Speed – the Car has Passed* 1913, oil on canvas, 50.2 x 65.4, Tate

Ballà was a leader of the group. He believed that the power and speed of machines were the most important features of modern life and aimed to express this idea in his work. This painting was originally the right-hand part of a triptych. The left-hand part was called *Line of Force + Landscape* and the central one *Lines of Force + Noise*. The theme was the passage of a car along a white road, with green and blue shapes, suggesting earth and sky in the background. The pinkish areas indicate the exhaust fumes left by the passing car.

39

The Vorticists were a British avant-garde group formed in London in around 1914 by the artist and writer Wyndham Lewis (1882–1957). Their only group exhibition was held in London in 1915 and they produced two issues of a magazine called *Blast*, which contained two aggressive manifestos by Lewis 'blasting' what he saw as the self-indulgence of British art. Like several other modern movements at the time, Vorticism was practised by angry young men.

Fast and furious

Vorticism combined concepts from Cubism and Futurism to express the dynamism of the modern world. It differed from Futurism in the way the artists' conveyed movement. In Vorticist paintings, modern life is shown in bold lines and harsh colours drawing the viewer's eye into the centre of the canvas. Some artists and writers associated with the movement included Ezra Pound (1885–1972), who named the movement, Henri Gaudier-Brzeska (1891–1915), Jacob Epstein (1880–1959) and Jessica Dismorr (1885–1939). The painter David Bomberg (1890–1957) was not formally a member of the group, but he produced work in a similar style at the same time. The movement ended in 1915, because of the demands of the First World War and because the public was not interested in the work. Gaudier-Brzeska was killed in military service and other artists in the group changed their styles. Unsuccessfully, Wyndham Lewis attempted to revive the movement in the 1920s under the name 'Group X'.

CELEBRATING THE NEW

Try to imagine what it was like for the Vorticists and the Futurists:

- Museums only showed people old things from history; these young artists thought we should be thinking more about the future (they didn't yet know about the two world wars).
- Just like museums, libraries and churches were from the past, but cars, aeroplanes and machine guns were all new.
- Writers and composers had been admired for centuries, so wasn't it time that new professions, like entertainers, sportspeople and hairdressers, were treated like celebrities? (Remember, this was then).
- There's a bit of a conflict going on – these artists wanted to be admired and appreciated, but they also wanted to appear radical and ahead of their time.

David Bomberg, *In the Hold* c.1913–14, oil on canvas, 196.2 x 231.1, Tate
This painting shows Bomberg's search for a way to show his view of the modern urban environment. At first glance it is a kaleidoscope of shapes, but it is based on a real scene of dockworkers in the hold of a ship. Look for a ladder in deep blue in the lower right, leading from the hold to the deck above: a hand holds one of the lower rungs. In the centre left in lighter blue and white, one of the dockers wearing a hat stretches his arms across the canvas. This mosaic-like image represents the East End of London or the 'steel city' Bomberg said he lived in.

VORTICISM

'Revolution today is taken for granted, and in consequence becomes rather dull.'
Wyndham Lewis

Whose idea was it anyway?
An exhibition at the Tate Gallery in 1956 called
Wyndham Lewis and the Vorticists made other
members of the group angry as a comment by him
was printed in the exhibition catalogue: 'Vorticism,
in fact, was what I, personally, did, and said, at a
certain period.'

Jacob Epstein, *Torso in Metal from
'The Rock Drill'* 1913–14, bronze,
70.5 x 58.4 x 44.5, Tate
Epstein initially set an entire plaster
figure on top of an actual pneumatic rock
drill. Intimidating and menacing, it
looked like a robot wearing a visor and
became a symbol of the new machine
age. At one point Epstein even considered
adding a motor to make it move, but after
the First World War he removed the drill,
cut the figure to half-length and changed
its arms. Now the once-threatening
figure appears vulnerable, its armour
leaving part of the soft body showing –
almost a victim of modern life.

Orphism or Orphic Cubism was a term invented in France in 1912 by the poet Guillaume Apollinaire (1880–1918). He connected Delaunay's style of contrasting colours, shapes and light with the Greek mythological poet Orpheus who blended mysticism with magic. The name was also used in relation to Delaunay's wife, Sonia (1885–1979), Picabia, Duchamp, Franz Kupka (1871–1957) and Léger.

INNER AND OUTER VISION

- In mythology, Orpheus was a singer who tamed wild beasts with his music
- Delaunay said that work expressed visual sensations, inner feelings and rhythms like music
- Americans Morgan Russell (1886–1953) and Stanton Macdonald-Wright (1890–1973) said Orphism was 'just decoration'
- Robert Delaunay was incensed. His art, he said, was 'pure expression of form through colour'
- Apollinaire only used the term Orphism for about a year
- Initially the Orphists based their pictures on the real world but by 1912 their work was completely abstract
- Delaunay and Kupka were the first French artists to paint abstract works
- Orphism ended with the start of the First World War, but it influenced many other artists, including German Expressionists, Macke, Klee and Marc

Form through colour

Orphism contains elements of Cubist ideas, but the artists replaced form and tone with bright colours rather than muted ones. Artists represented the world around them, without trying to incorporate their emotions and without adding tone to try to make things appear as we see them. With overlapping planes of contrasting colours a lot of the work resembles colourful collages, but it was created in a calculated and considered way. Artists were more concerned with the expression and significance of sensations as we view things, so they still painted recognisable subjects but also included increasingly abstract arrangements. They aimed to gradually rely only on form and colour to communicate perceptions of the visual world. They judged colours carefully and precisely, in an approach similar to the Impressionists and Seurat, breaking down the way our eyes view things. As Cubism tried to show several planes and angles at once, so did Orphism, but it also reduced everything to almost flat geometric shapes and multiple layers of colour since it was more about colour and light than solidity.

Colour theories

'Simultanism' is a term invented by the Delaunays to describe the abstract painting they developed from about 1910. It derived from Michel Chevreul's theories published in 1839, particularly the 'law of simultaneous contrast of colours' which had an increasing impact on French painters, particularly the Impressionists, Post-Impressionists and Neo-Impressionists. The Delaunays' paintings consisted of interlocking or overlapping patches, or planes of contrasting (or complementary) colours. In Chevreul's theory, and in reality, contrasting colours placed together enhance each other, giving the painting greater intensity and vibrancy. The artists based their painting on the movements of the eye as we perceive things. Orphism ended at the onset of the First World War, but had significant influence on the development of later abstract art movements.

ORPHISM

'Vision is the true creative rhythm.'
Robert Delaunay

Opposite Robert Delaunay, *Champ de Mars: The Red Tower* 1911/23, oil on canvas, 160.7 x 128.6, The Art Institute of Chicago
Delaunay's compositions were often inspired by architecture, particularly views of the Eiffel Tower and other parts of Paris. He tried to break down the way people really see everything: that is, not still and in one piece, but in colourful parts as we move, focus and digest the information. Delaunay and the others were serious about colour optics, direct observation of the radiance of nature, how the human eye breaks down colour and light, and the movement of colours.

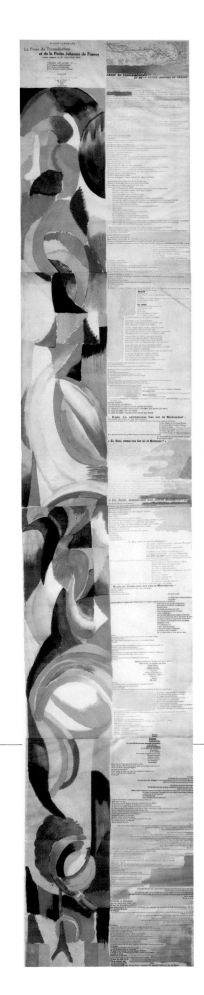

Right **Text by Blaise Cendrars, illustrated by Sonia Delaunay,** *Prose on the Trans-Siberian Railway and of Little Jehanne of France* **1913, watercolour and relief print on paper, 195.6 x 35.6, Tate**

Sonia Terk was a Ukrainian-French artist. She married Robert Delaunay in 1910 and the two became absorbed with optics, colour and geometric shapes. She developed her work in painting, textile design and stage set design, moving further away from perspective and naturalism as the years went by. In 1912 she met the poet Blaise Cendrars (1887–1961), who became a friend and collaborator, and she illustrated his poem 'La Prose du Transsibérien et de La Petite

Jehanne de France', about a journey on the Trans-Siberian Railway, in a two-metre long accordion-type book. Using the principles of simultaneous contrasts of colours (see p.16) the book merged text and design. Sold by subscription, it created a stir amongst Paris critics; after seeing it at an exhibition Paul Klee was so impressed with Sonia Delaunay's use of squares in the work that they became an enduring feature of his own work.

During the first decade of the 20th century Russia was still a Tsarist Empire under the rule of Nicholas II, while new developments in the world were changing the way people thought, such as Einstein's *Theory of Relativity*, the invention of the vacuum cleaner, the Model-T Ford and the assembly line. These influences were apparent in movements such as Futurism and Cubism, and the interest spread to Russia.

ART IN CONTEXT

THE RUSSIAN SITUATION

From 1892 until 1917 Russia experienced serious problems. During the 1890s and early 1900s, poverty, high taxes and lack of food generated discontentment and frequent strikes. By 1895 there were conflicts between Russia, Germany, Britain and Japan. On 9th January 1905 Russian workers petitioning against the Tsar were massacred in St Petersburg. This became known as 'Bloody Sunday' and was followed by strikes, demonstrations, vandalism, assassinations of government officials and further violence. In several cities workers formed 'Soviets' or councils. The unrest continued intermittently until the Russian Revolution of 1917 and the First World War. The Revolution involved the overthrow of the Tsar and the government, and eventually led to the establishment of the Soviet Union in 1922.

Out of the frame

You will by now have noticed that what goes on politically or religiously nearly always affects contemporary art. There was a great deal of unrest in Russia at the beginning of the 20th century, and two new art movements emerged. Suprematism was the name given by Kasimir Malevich (1878–1935) to the art he developed from 1913 where he attempted to represent the visual world without using any objects – so achieving 'pure art'. The first Suprematist exhibition, entitled *O.10*, was in St Petersburg in 1915. It included 35 paintings by Malevich, among them a black square painted on a white ground, which was hung in the manner of an icon. Suprematism was intended to supersede all other art forms. Rectangles, triangles and circles, often in intense colours and usually painted on white canvases with no frames, were intended to integrate with their surroundings. In 1919 El Lissitsky (1890–1941) met Malevich and was strongly influenced by Suprematism, as was Hungarian-born László Moholy-Nagy (1895–1946) and brothers Naum Gabo (1890–1977) and Antoine Pevsner (1886–1962), as well as Vladimir Tatlin (1885–1953).

Abstract structures

In 1913 Tatlin had seen Picasso's Cubist three-dimensional still lifes made of scrap materials and began to make his own, but they were completely abstract and made of industrial materials. Joined by Alexander Rodchenko (1891–1956) and other artists, they developed ideas from Cubism and Futurism, calling themselves Constructivists, and in 1921 they published a manifesto in their magazine, *Lef* (signifying the Left Front of the Arts – in Russian, 'Levyi Front Iskusstv'). Constructivism was one of the first movements to adopt strictly non-objective subject matter. Artists used only basic shapes, including squares, rectangles and circles, and materials such as wood, plastic, metal, cardboard and wire welded or glued together, to show the dominance of the machine in the modern world. When Joseph Stalin – one of the most powerful and murderous dictators in history – came to power in 1927 it became difficult for Suprematist and Constructivist artists in Russia to share their ideas with the Western world.

CONSTRUCTIVISM & SUPREMATISM

'Trying desperately to free art from the dead weight of the real world, I took refuge in the form of the square.'
Kasimir Malevich

Above Kasimir Malevich, *Dynamic Suprematism* 1915 or 1916, oil on canvas, 80.3 x 80, Tate

Malevich experimented extensively in the unsettled period leading up to the 1917 Russian Revolution. He abandoned representative images in favour of what he called Suprematism in 1915. Using drastically reduced geometric shapes – most famously his black square on a white canvas – he compared them to old religious icons. This painting demonstrates his irrepressible energy, as shapes mingle on the canvas without relying on any reference to the physical world.

Right Naum Gabo, *Head No. 2* 1916, enlarged version 1964, steel, 175.3 x 134 x 122.6, Tate

Associated with the Suprematists and the Constructivists, Gabo embraced new scientific theories and industrial materials. Using a method known as 'stereometric construction', he made constructions that show mass and structure, almost like skeletons without muscles and skin. From 1915 to 1920 he used planes to construct heads and figures to demonstrate the application of this method to traditional subjects. This is an enlargement of a model he had made nearly fifty years earlier, in 1916.

In 1916, appalled by the atrocities of the First World War, artists and writers from various countries moved to Zürich in neutral Switzerland. In a club called 'Cabaret Voltaire', they questioned how people who could produce beautiful art could also be so destructive, and they decided to shock society out of the attitudes that had led to the War in the first place.

The element of chance was important as they believed that everything had become pointless and damaged – there was no point trying to use skill or spend time creating anything of quality. Their poetry, for example, consisted of random word combinations, which they sometimes read out in public places. Some works of art were made of materials found by chance and arranged accidentally. They claimed that all their work was meaningless and disrespectable on purpose. The biggest difference about this art and art that had gone before was that it was more about ideas than anything else. The poet André Breton (1896–1966) said, 'Dada is a state of mind', meaning that it was more an attitude than an artistic trend.

Garbage pictures

Dada involved writers, actors and artists who staged cabarets, concerts, demonstrations and exhibitions. The artist Jean (or Hans) Arp (1886–1966) later wrote: 'Revolted by the butchery of the 1914 World War, we in Zürich devoted ourselves to the arts.' Soon, groups of Dadaists also formed in Paris, Hanover, Cologne, Berlin and New York.

Dada had no set style – everyone worked in different ways. In Cologne, for example, Max Ernst (1891–1976) exhibited a wooden sculpture with an axe attached. Why? So that viewers could chop the sculpture to bits if they fancied, of course. Some Dadaists made art out of rubbish. Arp made collages by gluing bits of torn or cut paper wherever it fell; Kurt Schwitters (1887–1948) made collages of objects he collected or found, such as old newspapers, tickets and wrappers. He called his collages 'Merz', which was part of a word on a piece of newspaper in one of his collages.

Readymades

Marcel Duchamp was initially interested in Futurism, but he moved on to Dada. He became known for the invention of 'readymades', works of art made of objects taken from everyday life with little or no intervention by the artist. Through readymades Duchamp was pointing out that objects become works of art when artists choose to display them.

Anti-art

The Dadaists always claimed that they were not creating art, they were un-creating it. It was therefore 'anti-art'. Ernst said: 'Dada has never claimed to have anything to do with art. If the public confuses the two, that is no fault of ours.'

NONSENSE NAME

The artists found a name for their protests by picking a word by chance from a dictionary. The word was 'dada' and they liked it because it meant several things and nothing much at the same time. In French, dada means 'hobbyhorse', in Russian it means 'yes, yes' and in most other languages it simply sounds like baby talk.

DADA

'A work of art is a corner of creation seen through a temperament.'
Émile Zola

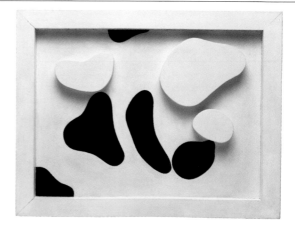

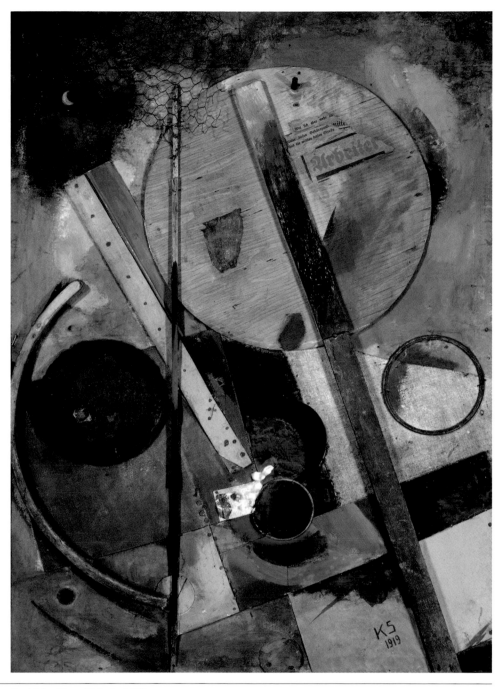

Opposite Jean (Hans) Arp, *Constellation According to the Laws of Chance* c.1930, painted wood, 54.9 x 69.8, Tate
Hans Arp felt that modern society was trying to understand things that should simply be accepted. He developed an art that suggested the forms and shapes of nature without trying to copy them or rationalise why he was doing it. The rounded shapes in this relief could suggest clouds or planets, while the laws of chance mean nature's unpredictability. Even the way he made his reliefs relied on chance: he ordered the pieces from a craftsman but only gave vague instructions, so as to encourage the craftsman's free interpretation.

Kurt Schwitters, '*Arbeiterbild*' (*Work Picture*) 1919, found objects on board, 125 x 91, National Art Museums Collection, Sweden
Nonsense was a key element in Schwitters' work. For this he randomly stuck down odd scraps and named it *Arbeiter* after a word he could see on the board. He was mocking the seriousness of traditional art while representing the rubbish that we all create.

47

The Dadaists' experiments were conceptual and confident and paved the way for later artists to be more daring. Duchamp's ideas were some of the boldest. In 1913 he produced the first 'readymade', his name for mass-produced objects he found and left unaltered before giving each a title and signature (see p.46). He described each readymade as 'a work of art without an artist to make it'.

Strong feelings

Challenging aesthetic values and stimulating discussion about artistic processes and art marketing, Duchamp aroused strong feelings. Some people thought his work was offensive and insulting to 'real' art, even though he was pointing out that things can be appreciated even if they are not created for their beauty. Some people liked the irony of presenting such things as works of art. Duchamp produced relatively few artworks, yet thousands of books and articles have attempted to interpret his art and philosophy; but in interviews and his writing he only added to the mystery. Many of his ideas had considerable influence on the development of Western art, and he advised art collectors, which helped to shape the tastes of the Western art world.

WHAT'S THE JOKE?

So what were Duchamp and Picabia up to when they were ridiculing art? Where were they going with their jokes and puns? Wasn't it all a bit bad taste? Well, yes it was. Their point was to create art that shocked the public and did not adhere to good taste. Irritated by the arrogance of the art world, they both dismissed the idea of joining a particular group and introduced jokes into their art to try to jolly things up. The debate over whether it was art at all continues to this day.

DUCHAMP & PICABIA

'I am interested in ideas, not merely in visual products.'
Marcel Duchamp

Francis Picabia, *The Fig-Leaf* 1922, oil on canvas, 200 x 160, Tate
One of the major Dada figures, French artist and writer Picabia painted this using household gloss paint over an earlier painting. He was irritated at the way in which artists were expected to conform to what was acceptable; his stand against conventionality helped subsequent generations of artists to be more innovative. The figure in this painting is 'borrowed' from an earlier painting by Ingres, with Picabia's addition of a fig-leaf as a reference to restrictions on artists. The inscription 'dessin français' (French drawing) ridiculed traditional art skills.

A man for all styles

Francis-Marie Martinez Picabia had a traditional art education in Paris. At first he was influenced by the Impressionist Alfred Sisley (1839–99) and later by Cubism. Around 1911 he joined the Puteaux Group, a discussion group in the French village of Puteaux organised by Duchamp and his two older brothers, artists Jacques Villon (1875–1963) and Raymond Duchamp-Villon (1876–1918). There Picabia became a friend of Duchamp and others including Delaunay and Léger, and he exhibited work inspired by Cubism and Orphism. He travelled to New York several times between 1913 and 1917, where he met Man Ray (1890–1976) and Alfred Stieglitz (1864–1946), who were pioneers in avant-garde art and photography. His artistic protests against traditional values helped later artists to be more pioneering. His paintings and drawings of machines in 'colour harmonies' were criticised in the press as 'a danger to art', even when he explained that he 'put his soul on canvas' and attempted 'to express the purest part of the abstract reality of form and colour'.

In 1916 Picabia published his Dada periodical *391*, with Duchamp's help, featuring some of his mechanical drawings. He continued his involvement in the Dada movement throughout the First World War and until 1924, when he associated with the Surrealists. By 1926, though, he moved to the South of France and began to paint in aggressive, bright colours. Some of these works, inspired by Romanesque frescoes, he called 'transparencies' as they involved several translucent layers of paint. During the 1940s Picabia produced a series of paintings of nudes in a brash style which undermine conventional academic nude painting. Back in Paris before the end of the Second World War, he painted dancers with whom he had love affairs and also produced 'dot pictures', which he had designed from microscopic images of plants.

Marcel Duchamp, *Fountain* 1917, replica 1964, readymade, Tate
Duchamp's most notorious readymade was a urinal that he turned upside down, labelled *Fountain* and signed 'R. Mutt', the name of a toilet manufacturing company. It began as a joke and he put it in an exhibition where there was no jury so no one could turn it away, but the other exhibitors hid it! Duchamp's point was that technical skill is not essential and art does not have to be unique.

Marc Chagall (1887–1985) treated his subjects with humour and fantasy, exploring the unconscious as well as personal ideas and memories. Born in Vitebsk (now Belarus) in Russia to a religious Jewish family, he trained as an artist from an early age. In his early twenties he moved to Paris and met Apollinaire, Delaunay, Léger, Amedeo Modigliani (1884–1920) and André Lhote (1885–1962). Chagall was influenced by Cubism, but mixed it with his own type of fantasy. He returned to Russia in 1914 for the duration of the First World War. After the Russian Revolution of 1917 he produced murals for a Jewish theatre in Moscow, was appointed Fine Arts Commissar for the province of Vitebsk and founded an art school there. His work depicts vivid incidents in his life, while his imaginary paintings commemorate the Russia of his youth and his Jewish ancestors. From 1923 he spent most of his life in France, except for a short time in America from 1941 to 1948.

Pittura metafisica

Giorgio de Chirico (1888–1978) was a painter, sculptor, theatrical designer and writer, born in Greece to Italian parents. He studied drawing and painting in Greece, Germany and Italy, moving to Paris around 1911, where he met Apollinaire, Picasso and the Symbolist painter Arnold Böcklin (1827–1901) among others. From about 1915 he began producing a series of menacing cityscapes, which were highly praised by painters and poets. He called this phase the *pittura metafisica*, meaning metaphysical art or dreamlike pictures. Many of the places he painted were inspired by locations in Italy, such as Turin and Ferrara. The Surrealists admired de Chirico's early work but attacked him after 1958 when he adopted a more traditional style. He spent the 1930s in Italy, Paris and New York, and settled in Rome in 1943. He later designed sets and costumes for various ballets and operas, and also made a number of small sculptures.

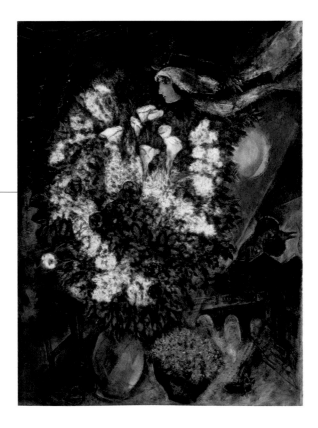

ART IN CONTEXT

PAINTING DREAMS

Dreams and memories are subjects that painters and writers return to over and again. Modern artists broke all existing rules of art to create their own imaginative representations of reality, believing that they could not show the depths of emotion they felt with traditional art.

CHAGALL & DE CHIRICO

'If I create from the heart, nearly everything works; if from the head, almost nothing.'
Marc Chagall

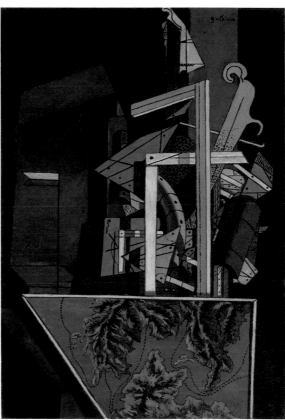

Opposite **Marc Chagall**, *Bouquet with Flying Lovers* c.1934–47, oil on canvas, 130.5 x 97.5, Tate

Chagall's works combine his memories with folklore and fantasy. He began this painting in the mid-1930s, when he was living in Paris. He worked on it at intervals over many years and the final composition included several changes. Two lovers hover behind the flowers, while an angel flies in through the window. To the right is a glimpse of Chagall's birthplace, the village of Vitebsk. The painting seems to suggest a happy atmosphere, but Chagall said that it expressed feelings of loss and nostalgia: his wife Bella died shortly before he completed it.

Giorgio de Chirico, *The Uncertainty of the Poet* 1913, oil on canvas, 106 x 94, Tate

The quiet square suggests the classical arcades and antique sculpture of Italy and Greece. In contrast, the passing train and perishable bananas suggest a sense of the contemporary and immediate. The distorted perspective and shadows are unexpected and threatening, creating a dreamlike image which inspired many of the Surrealists.

Giorgio de Chirico, *The Melancholy of Departure* 1916, oil on canvas, 51.8 x 35.9, Tate

The window and the map with a traced route evoke ideas of travel, suggesting escape from a cluttered, claustrophobic studio. As a child in Greece, de Chirico felt detached from his surroundings and identified with the voyaging Argonauts of Greek mythology, imagining their journey across 'measureless oceans.' *The Melancholy of Departure* was painted after he had returned from Paris to Italy to serve in the First World War.

In the Netherlands in 1917 the painters Mondrian and van Doesburg and architect and designer Gerrit Rietveld (1888–1964) founded the art and design movement De Stijl (the Style). Mondrian was the main advocate, and he invented his own 'ism', Neo-Plasticism, describing painting as a plastic, or flexible, art form.

ART IN CONTEXT

GEOMETRIC BALANCE

Before you jump to conclusions, try to see things from Mondrian's perspective. He said:

- He wanted no distracting elements or associations
- His goal was pure reality, without any diversions
- He was trying to achieve balance, rhythm and harmony above all things
- He reached his compositions by feel and a sense of geometric balance

Not convinced? Try producing your own version and see if yours is as balanced and complete-looking as his.

DE STIJL

'The position of the artist is humble. He is essentially a channel.'
Piet Mondrian

What's the angle?

These artists were aiming for total abstraction, using only straight lines and right angles. They limited their palettes to the three primary colours, red, yellow and blue, and the three non-colours, black, white and grey. As they developed, De Stijl artists dispensed with anything that suggested an object or anything from the visible world. Their compositions were completely simplified: painted surfaces were smooth and without visible brushwork, and lines were always straight and perpendicular to each other. They were trying to reach viewers in a spiritual way – to make people think of things other than the material world. This was rather self-conscious, and certainly odd for the time (the First World War was raging) but the artists persevered. In the end Mondrian fell out with van Doesburg for including diagonals in his painting. What a nerve.

Influences

Mondrian and the others had looked at Cubism and realised that it was a clever idea, but they didn't think it was quite there yet. Mondrian was also influenced by the complex spiritual ideas of Theosophy, so his paintings try to offer inner harmony, rejecting the subjectivity of individual artists and the world around them. The fact that they were working during the First World War, when the countries of the Western world were destroying each other, had a big effect on the way these artists were thinking and viewing the world at the time. De Stijl magazine spread the word about trying to attain harmony and balance in a damaged world. Remember that many of these artists were not humourless and a lot of their work was not intended to be taken deadly seriously.

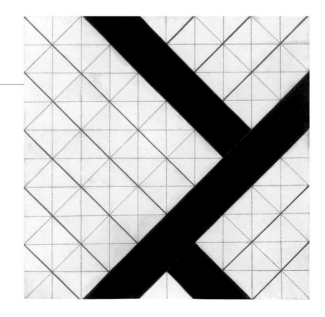

Along with Kandinsky and Mondrian, Malevich (see pp.44–5) is one of the pioneers of abstract art, even though he is only known for about thirty paintings and drawings. His early works were inspired by Impressionism and Post-Impressionism, but he soon began thinking that art should be quite separate from nature. For this reason – because they do not exist in nature – he painted geometric forms. As nothing is recognisable from the world in his paintings, Malevich forces his viewer to respond to each work on an instinctive level, without making any associations with the visible world at all. In their own areas, Malevich, Kandinsky and Mondrian were trying to encourage spiritual contemplation. Before you scoff, remember two things:

- the works in this book are smaller and lack the textures of the real thing, so you really need to see them if you can, and
- the works you see here have been copied and adapted hundreds of times in countless ways since they were first produced by the original artists. When they were first created, no one else had done anything like them.

Flat colour

Mondrian's grid-like paintings came from his belief that the universe is made up of opposites – dark and light, male and female, coloured and colourless. He spent a great deal of his life in Paris, New York and London and he exhibited with other De Stijl artists in Paris in 1923. He withdrew from the group after van Doesburg reintroduced diagonal elements into his work around 1925. He carried on evolving his style, although the refinements became more subtle. He saw subject matter as an impurity that limited the broadness and scope of a painting by tying it to a particular time and place. His search for absolute order can be paralleled with the ancient Egyptians, who also produced compositions with grids, emphasised the flatness of their surfaces and wanted their paintings to be timeless and eternal. The Second World War forced Mondrian to move to London in 1938, and then, in October 1940, to settle in New York. Here he joined the American Abstract Artists and continued writing and publishing texts on Neo-Plasticism.

DOES IT WORK?

If you get an opportunity to see any of these abstract works, don't try to associate them with anything you've seen before. Look at each work, relax, don't talk and try not to think of anything in particular. What do you feel or think of?

Kasimir Malevich, *Suprematist Composition* c.1916, oil on canvas, 53 x 53, Peggy Guggenheim Collection, Venice
By combining geometric forms and juxtaposing planes of pure colour, Malevich applied ideas similar to those of De Stijl (pp.52–3), before that movement began. He used regular shapes, which seem almost opposite to the flowing feelings of mysticism he wanted to inspire.

MALEVICH & MONDRIAN

'By "Suprematism" I mean the supremacy of pure feeling in creative art.'
Kasimir Malevich

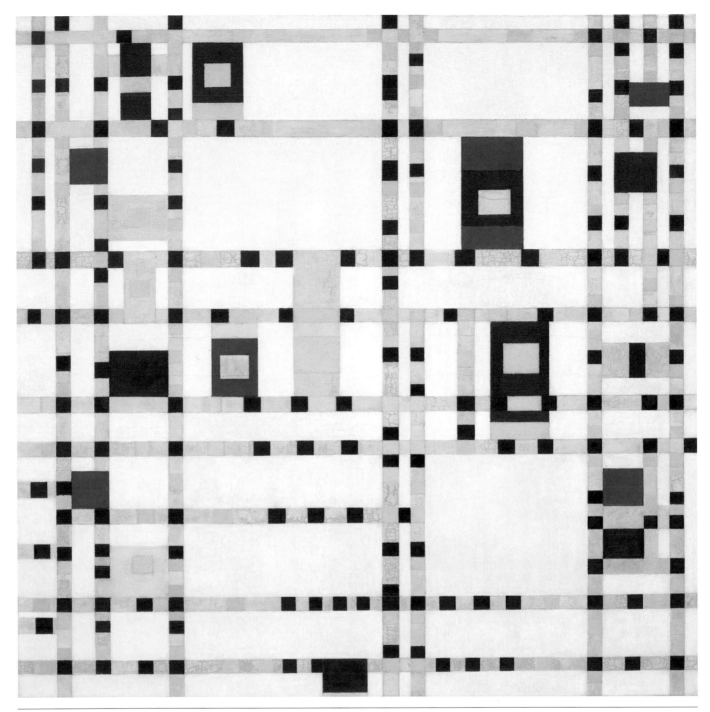

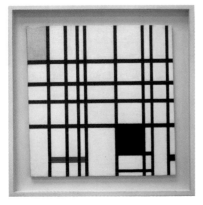

Left Piet Mondrian, *Composition with Yellow, Blue and Red* 1937–42, oil on canvas, 72.7 x 69.2, Tate

First of all Mondrian painted his canvas white, and then he marked on the black grid-lines. Primary colours were added to balance and simplify the spiritual experience. Balance didn't necessarily mean symmetry, however: the structure is asymmetrical, reflecting the vibrant balance of true life.

Above Piet Mondrian, *Broadway Boogie Woogie* 1942–3, oil on canvas, 127 x 127, **Museum of Modern Art, New York**

Mondrian's late style evolved in response to the city of New York where he was living during the Second World War. He loved dancing and jazz music, and tried to incorporate their rhythms in this work. This painting was highly influential with other abstract artists, made up of a number of squares of bright colour that appear to shimmer and move, like little cars moving along a busy street or the blinking electric street lights. Here Mondrian has broken the black bands of his earlier work into multicoloured strips, creating an optical vibration.

Traditional paintings and sculpture and films about war often emphasise the courage and action involved, but modern artists turned against this emphasis on heroics and glorifying war. Abhorring its destruction, horror and inhumanity, they created art that focused on the terror, tragedy and waste of life.

No longer being paid to produce art by rulers who wanted to celebrate victories or to encourage patriotism, many modern artists have produced personal points of view, giving more accurate, bleaker images. We've already looked at several of these, from the Dadaists (pp.46–9) and the Vorticists (pp.40–41) to Picasso's *Weeping Woman* (p.30) and Kandinsky's *Battle* (p.17). Although all these artists wished to portray their repugnance, not all created actual images of war. Some used other forms of symbolism or expression, created to reinforce ideas of disgust and loathing at needless destruction and deaths.

From the trenches

Paul Nash (1889–1946) was born in London. At the Slade School of Art, where he trained in landscape painting, he met Stanley Spencer (1891–1959) and Mark Gertler (1891–1939), among others. With the outbreak of the First World War Nash joined the Artists' Rifles and was sent to fight in Northern France. Whenever possible he sketched life in the trenches. In 1917 he was sent home after an accident and while recuperating he produced a series of war paintings. He was appointed Official War Artist later that year, and again twenty years later, during the Second World War.

Stanley Spencer served in the First World War, from 1915 to 1918, painting detailed and objective images in a simplified, naïve style, but varying his approach and manner according to the assignment. After the First and during the Second World War Spencer, like his friend Paul Nash, was commissioned by the government to paint images of what he had experienced.

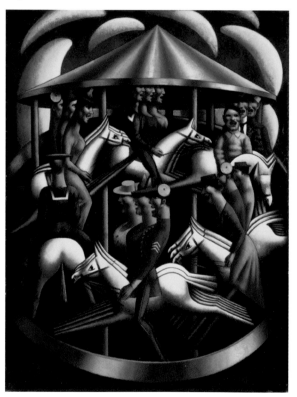

Mark Gertler, *Merry-Go-Round* 1916, oil on canvas, 210 x 162, Tate
Painted at the height of the First World War, this shows men and women in uniform, sitting rigidly, seemingly trapped on a carousel that should be fun but, as shown by their screaming faces, is terrifying. Gertler may have been inspired by a fair that was held annually for wounded soldiers near his home. The composition pushes the figures forward and the harsh colours emphasise the disturbing atmosphere.

WAR & DESTRUCTION

'War! That mad game the world so loves to play.'
Jonathan Swift

Top Paul Nash, *Totes Meer (Dead Sea)* **1940–1, oil on canvas, 101.6 x 152.4, Tate**
After his eyes were opened to the horrors of war, Nash adopted the angular avant-garde styles of Cubism and Vorticism and painted powerful and terrifying landscapes of death on the battlefields. This painting was inspired by abandoned, wrecked aircraft: Nash is showing there can be no hope of coming back alive from such a place, which has become a field of death. Basing the image on photographs he took on the Western Front, Nash said: 'The thing looked to me suddenly, like a great inundating sea ... and then, nothing moves, it is not water or even ice, it is something static and dead.'

Bottom Stanley Spencer, *Travoys Arriving with Wounded at a Dressing Station at Smol, Macedonia, September 1916* **1919, oil on canvas, 182.8 x 218.4, Imperial War Museum, London**
On the outbreak of the First World War Spencer joined the Royal Army Medical Corps. In 1918 he was asked to contribute a picture about his experiences to the British government's Hall of Remembrance; this was the painting he produced, in 1919. Viewed from above, blanket-wrapped wounded soldiers on stretchers (travoys) are pulled by mules towards an operating theatre. Although the location has a name, the simplified perspective and colours, plus the

anonymity of all the figures, imply that it stands for any or all of the young men who fought in the War. There is order and calm, perhaps showing that Spencer (a devout Christian) believed that the dead had now found peace.

The Bauhaus was an art school that became a huge art and design movement. It emerged as architects and artists began to rebuild a battle-torn Europe after the First World War, and became a fashion in itself. Its influence on design, including architecture, furniture, typography and household objects, has affected the look of our modern environment more than many people realise.

Creating a better environment

A year after the end of the First World War in Weimar, Germany, the architect Walter Gropius (1883–1969) joined two art schools together and called the result 'Bauhaus', meaning 'House of Building.' Many famous avant-garde artists and designers taught there, including Kandinsky, Klee, Moholy-Nagy, Marcel Breuer (1902–81) and van Doesburg. With similar ideas to the De Stijl group, artists and designers at the Bauhaus thought they could create a better environment. This followed on from ideas introduced by the 19th-century designer William Morris (1834–96), who advised: 'Have nothing in your house that you do not know to be useful, or believe to be beautiful.' The notion of excluding all unattractive objects, unless they serve a useful function, is now known to raise both standards and self-esteem.

Clean lines

The Bauhaus taught fine arts and crafts and from the start encouraged students to leave out unnecessary ornamentation or fussiness. Teaching in every department focused on creating harmonious designs with clean lines and functional craftsmanship, and students were encouraged to design with mass-produced goods in mind. Unlike any other art school, the Bauhaus taught students the basics of all crafts and art before they specialised in a subject of their choice. The curriculum that developed became the standard for many subsequent European and American art schools – and was the forerunner to the foundation course taken by most art students in Britain today before beginning an art or design degree. Another unique aspect of the Bauhaus was that skilled craftsmen instructed the students in the use of tools and techniques in manipulating various materials, teaching alongside gifted artists who provided insights into concepts of form and design.

These ideas were extremely controversial and unpopular in Weimar, so in 1925 the school moved to the town of Dessau. Here the close association of many Bauhaus teachers and students with socialist ideas made the school the object of attack by right-wingers and the fascists. In September 1932 it was forced to move again, this time to Berlin, where it existed briefly until it was closed by the Nazis in April 1933.

FACTS IN A FRAME

MANY DISCIPLINES

Students at the Bauhaus studied painting and design, along with craft skills such as woodwork, weaving and pottery. Gropius was trying to obscure the traditional distinction between arts and crafts, encouraging his students to create stylish and practical objects and to learn about industrial processes.

THE BAUHAUS 1919–33

*'Art does not reproduce what we see;
rather, it makes us see.'*
Paul Klee

Paul Klee, *They're Biting* 1920, drawing and oil on paper, 31.1 x 23.5, Tate
Klee painted free images, often linking them with music, and remained fascinated by children's painting. He believed that there was another world, more real than this one and his work and ideas reflected this. This painting is a kind of fantasy world, where fish are responding to the fisherman's hook with punctuation marks indicating their surprise.

Marcel Breuer, *Wassily Chair* 1927–8, chrome-plated tubular steel and canvas, 71.8 x 78.1 x 71.1, Museum of Modern Art, New York
While teaching at the Bauhaus, Breuer made this chair for his friend and colleague Kandinsky. Inspired by a bicycle, the frame was originally made from bent tubular steel but was later chrome-plated, while the seat and back are made from canvas, fabric or leather. Its use of tubular steel was revolutionary at the time. As it is affordable, hygienic and provides comfort without the need for springs, Breuer designed a whole range of tubular metal furniture, including chairs, tables, stools and cupboards.

During the first two decades of the 20th century, Latin American painters in Mexico became aware of movements such as Impressionism, Post-Impressionism, Symbolism and Art Nouveau.

For the people

The Mexican Revolution inspired artists to paint massive murals. These artists became known as the Mexican muralists and they used realism, touched with other influences, to make art more accessible to the public so that the problems faced by Mexican society were there for all to see. The three main muralists were Diego Rivera (1886–1957), José Clemente Orozco (1883–1949), and David Alfano Siqueiros (1896–1974), and they had varying political beliefs, personal temperaments and artistic styles. Their murals were commissioned to be in some of the most important buildings in Mexico: as public art they were painted for the all to see, rather than being hidden away for the benefit of a few.

FACTS IN A FRAME

REVOLUTION!

Throughout its history Mexico has had many revolutions. The most famous is the Mexican Revolution of 1910–20. For most of the country's developing history a small minority of the people were in control of most of the country's power and wealth, while the rest worked in poverty. Peasants resented rich citizens getting richer and more powerful while they had nothing, and the dictatorial President Porfirio Díaz was deeply unpopular. Civil unrest turned to revolution as people joined together to fight for social reform and freedom from poverty.

MEXICAN MURALISM

'I've never believed in God, but I believe in Picasso.'
Diego Rivera

Influence and impact

Influenced by European Modernism, Rivera studied in Spain and Paris and worked with Spanish artists Pablo Picasso and Juan Gris, who were experimenting with Cubism at the time. Rivera used Cubist techniques such as the use of a diagonal grid as the underlying structure in his paintings. He was also inspired by pre-Columbian and traditional Mexican folk art in his murals for the National Palace in Mexico City. Some pre-Columbian cultures, such as the Mexican Maya, painted frescoes and murals to record their daily life and depict historical events. Late 19th-century artist Paul Gauguin was also a significant influence – indeed, almost every European art movement from Impressionism and Symbolism made some kind of an impact among the painters and sculptors of Latin America. Constructivism and Expressionism had special importance too. Siqueiros and Orozco painted sensitive images expressing their sympathy with workers in pictures illustrating Mexican history. In the 1930s and 1940s Rivera, Orozco and Siqueiros all worked in the United States, where they influenced public art projects as well as the early work of American Abstract Expressionist Jackson Pollock (1912–56; see p.76–7).

Bottom **Diego Rivera,** *Dream of a Sunday Afternoon in Alameda Park* **1947–8, fresco, 480 x 1500, Diego Rivera Mural Museum, Mexico City**

This mural shows a Sunday afternoon in a Mexican park built on the grounds of an ancient Aztec marketplace. Illustrating the history of Mexico through symbolism and folklore, it depicts Rivera as a boy, holding hands with a female skeleton from a Mexican legend; the characters surrounding them symbolise significant events. But the mural was kept covered at first because Rivera had added the slogan 'God Does Not Exist'. Later, to proclaim his reconciliation with the Church, he painted out the offending words.

Top **José Clemente Orozco,** *Zapata* **1930, oil on canvas, 178.4 x 122.6, The Art Institute of Chicago**

Skilful, but physically handicapped and shy, Orozco had little formal art education. This is one of his many canvas paintings and it is as strong as some of the vast murals for which he became famous. It shows Emiliano Zapata (1879–1919), a leader of a peasant army who fought for the freedom of the poor, silhouetted against a doorway. He stands in front of two armed revolutionaries and two peasants with a sword pointing threateningly towards his face. After his assassination, Zapata became a symbol of the Revolution for many Mexicans.

Some artists fit into some categories and some fit into others; several overlap into various movements and styles. This book can only give you a taste of some of the art that has been produced since the beginning of the 20th century. Two artists who were influenced by the moods and styles of their time, but can't be defined by any particular art movements, are Frida Kahlo (1907–54) and Tamara de Lempicka (1898–1980).

KAHLO & DE LEMPICKA

'I never paint dreams or nightmares.
I paint my own reality.'
Frida Kahlo

Painful symbolism

Kahlo was Diego Rivera's wife and is now regarded as one of the most significant artists of the 20th century. Many of her works are self-portraits that symbolically express her own pain and low self-image. After surviving many traumas, including contracting polio as a child (which left her with a withered leg), a long recovery from a serious car accident, two failed marriages and several miscarriages, she used these experiences to create highly personal paintings. Her painting, using vibrant colours, shows strong Mexican and Native American cultural influences as well as that of some European styles, such as Symbolism and Surrealism. The small scale of most of her work is a result of being confined, often in a hospital bed. The stormy relationship she had with Rivera inspired many of her paintings. Drawing on personal experiences, her works range in mood from painful to pitiful to peaceful, depending on what was happening to her at the time. Of her 143 paintings, 55 are self-portraits which often incorporate symbolic portrayals of her physical and psychological pain. In 1939, at the invitation of the Surrealist poet André Breton (see p.46), she went to France and her work was featured at an exhibition in Paris; however, Kahlo always insisted that she was never a Surrealist.

Soft Cubism

Tamara de Lempicka became probably the most famous painter of the Art Deco period, after a romantic and mysterious beginning when she fled to Paris with her husband after the Russian Revolution. Influenced by the Cubist experiments of Braque, Gris and Picasso, her distinctive and bold artistic style developed quickly and was given the nickname 'Soft Cubism'. She believed that many of the Impressionists drew badly and used 'dirty' colours; by contrast, her colours and tones were clean, precise and elegant. In 1925 she exhibited her works at the first Art Deco show in Paris. She was soon the most fashionable portrait painter of her generation, although she was criticised as well as being admired. She moved to America in 1939.

Frida Kahlo, *Self-portrait with Monkey* 1938, oil on canvas, 40.6 x 30.5, Albright-Knox Art Gallery, New York
Repeatedly painting her own image, Kahlo explored her identity as a woman, artist, Mexican, disabled person and political activist. The naïve style, bright and bizarre colours and dramatic images reflect her love of Mexican art. In Mexican mythology, monkeys implied lust, yet Kahlo used them as protective symbols. Here, the monkey's arm is stretched round her neck, perhaps replacing the children she never had in her affections. Her self-portraits could be compared to religious icons: in this her characteristic features are impassively hiding her feelings.

ART DECO

Named after the *International Exhibition of Modern Decorative and Industrial Arts* held in Paris in 1925, Art Deco was a reaction against Art Nouveau (see p.20). The style was influenced by Cubism and Ancient Egyptian art (in 1922 the tomb of Tutankhamun had just been discovered), giving Art Deco design an angular, streamlined style. The style was also influenced by the design of modern ships, trains and cars, as well as drawing on the modern architecture and the design of the Bauhaus.

Tamara de Lempicka, *Young Girl in Green* 1929, oil on canvas, 61.5 x 45.5, Musée national d'art moderne, Paris
Painted in the soft, angular style that made de Lempicka famous, this figure reflects the glamorous side of society that existed in some places between the two world wars, and epitomises the Art Deco style. Tones and colours are clean and contrasting and the figure dominates the composition.

In case you think that modern art was all about being angry over wars and revolutions, here's a movement that was about, well, being angry – but not in the same way, and the resulting art was uplifting and fun. It became a celebration of a culture that had been stifled, but that was also developing in a new way through outside influences. Between 1920 and 1930, in a part of New York City, an outburst of creative activity among African-Americans occurred in all fields of art, including music, dance, film, theatre and cabaret.

Celebrating heritage

The movement became known as the Harlem Renaissance, but originally it was called the 'New Negro Movement' after art historian Alain Locke's book *The New Negro* of 1925, which urged black artists to look back to their ancestral heritage and so strengthen their own expression. At the time Harlem in New York City attracted prosperous and stylish black middle-class people, from which sprang an extraordinary artistic centre. Artists and writers celebrated their creativity and expressed themselves in a manner befitting their culture. They explored their identities as black Americans, celebrating both the ways they had developed since emerging out of slavery and also their cultural ties to Africa.

Several factors contributed to this movement, including racial unrest that developed from lynch mobs in the South and race riots in 25 cities in 1919. Prior to this, around 1916, cheap immigrant labour on southern farms stopped because of the First World War and many black people moved from the South to the North to find jobs in what became known as the Great Migration. From 1919 to 1926, hundreds of thousands of African-Americans moved to places like New York City, Chicago and Washington, DC. In addition, Afro-Caribbean artists and intellectuals from the British West Indies became part of the movement, and many French-speaking black writers from African and Caribbean colonies who lived in Paris were also influenced by it. Historians disagree about the start and end of the movement. Unofficially, it is recognised to have spanned from about 1919 until the early or mid-1930s, although its ideas continued for much longer.

Mixing styles, limiting palettes

Among the many artists, Aaron Douglas (1898–1979) painted murals for public buildings and produced illustrations and cover designs for many publications, including the two main Harlem Renaissance magazines, *The Crisis* and *Opportunity*. William H. Johnson (1901–70) arrived in Harlem in 1918 from South Carolina and was the first American artist of African descent to receive sustained mainstream recognition in the United States. Using a limited, bright palette, he mixed Modernism, primitive art and African-American life, flattening his figures in scenes of daily life.

JAZZY STYLE

Harlem nightlife, with its popular dance halls and jazz bands, featured prominently in their work. Harlem was always an important centre for jazz, which was developed during the 1920s by African-Americans.

HARLEM RENAISSANCE

'Our problem is to conceive, develop and establish an art era ... Let's do the impossible. Let's create something transcendentally material, mystically objective.'
Aaron Douglas

Top William H. Johnson, *Going to Church* 1940–1, oil on burlap, 96.5 x 115.5, Smithsonian American Art Museum, Washington, DC

Painting on rough cloth similar to sacking, here Johnson portrays the African-American community in a simple, 'folk' style of painting. He depicts religion as part of life's routine, reminding new communities of their past. As in van Gogh's *Bedroom at Arles* 1888 or the Biblical story of Adam and Eve, for instance, he includes pairs wherever possible: two trees, two blue buildings, two crosses, two cartwheels, two pairs of people and so on.

Bottom Aaron Douglas, *Aspects of Negro Life: From Slavery Through Reconstruction* 1934, oil on canvas, 152.4 x 353.1 , Schomburg Centre for Research in Black Culture, The New York Public Library

This is one of five murals for a branch of the New York Public Library. The murals depict the history of African-Americans, from their origins in Africa to life in America in the 1930s. Through his use of Egyptian, African and American art, Douglas created a fusion of ancient and modern styles. He emphasised design rather than realistic representation, with flat colours and figures evoking rhythms inspired by his background.

Surrealism was as rebellious as Dada (see pp.46–9), but more organised. At the beginning of the 20th century the study of psychology – the workings of the mind – was developing. In 1919 Dr Sigmund Freud (1856–1939) published a book called *The Interpretation of Dreams*, which claimed that dreams symbolically express our underlying desires. Freud identified a part of the human mind where memories and our most basic instincts are stored and, because we are mostly unaware of it, called it the unconscious. This book became central to the Surrealist movement. Surrealism had a huge influence on art, literature and the cinema, as well as on social attitudes.

Eerie and disturbing

The Surrealist artists adopted various techniques to unlock the unconscious mind, casting aside traditional methods of creating art and challenging usual ways of production. Some of their works are eerie and disturbing, while others are funny. Many subsequent literary and visual movements which challenge conventions have been influenced by Surrealism.

Two directions

The Surrealists followed two main routes. Max Ernst, Salvador Dalí (1904–89) and René Magritte (1898–1967) all painted dream-like images: technically skilful, their works are often illogical. Dalí called his pictures 'hand-painted dream photographs'. His behaviour was as surreal as his work – he once said, 'The only difference between me and a madman is that I am not mad'. And he once gave a lecture on Surrealism dressed in a deep-sea diving suit. In 1939 Dalí declared his support for the Spanish dictator General Franco and was expelled from the Surrealist group.

The second style of Surrealism was Automatism, the Surrealist term for Freud's technique of free association, which he used to reveal the unconscious minds of his patients. Joan Miró (1893–1983) and André Masson (1896–1987) were among those who practised Automatism, which meant working instinctively: not thinking about what was being created, but letting the unconscious take over. Any material could be used and the resulting colours and shapes should express underlying feelings and emotions. (Try it!) Miró claimed that he often starved himself in order to bring on hallucinations as he worked. (Don't try *that*.)

SURREALISM

'To be a Surrealist means barring from your mind all remembrance of what you have seen and being always on the lookout for what has never been.'
René Magritte

Opposite René Magritte, *Ceci n'est pas une pipe* 1928–9, oil on canvas, 63.5 x 93.9, Los Angeles County Museum of Art, California
Hands up if you thought this was a pipe. Wrong! Look again: it's not a pipe, it's a *painting* of a pipe! Magritte showed the world that we should not take all we see for granted. Once again, this is the art of ideas, showing us that we should not always believe in illusions. Magritte said: 'Just try to stuff it with tobacco! If I were to have had written on my picture "This is a pipe" I would have been lying.'

Top Joan Miró, *Carnival of Harlequin* 1924–5, oil on canvas, 66 x 90.5, Albright-Knox Art Gallery, New York
The background beige suggests the walls of a room. Through a window are sky and a mountain. Weightless creatures change shape and position, as dream images often do. The distorted animal forms, twisted shapes and odd geometric constructions are painted in a limited range of bright colours, mingled with sharp lines, spots and curls. In Miró's mind the carnival has entered the room.

Bottom Salvador Dalí, *Autumnal Cannibalism* 1936, oil on canvas, 65.1 x 65.1, Tate
Painted during the Spanish Civil War, this represents the people attacking each other. The background is a Spanish landscape and in the foreground are two deformed, melting figures on an empty chest of drawers, eating each other. The figure on the left is a woman; the other is a man. Dalí was comparing the pain of one nation fighting itself with relationships between men and women. Here, both the war and male and female relationships are blind and helpless, with no faces and no bones.

Although most of the artists considered so far have been painters, several influential artists in modern art movements have been architects or designers or sculptors. Sculptors have traditionally joined in with art movements, but remained on the fringe. Three respected sculptors who became part of avant-garde groups and movements without being tied to them, and essentially did their own thing independently, are Henry Moore (1898–1986), Barbara Hepworth and Louise Bourgeois (born 1911). Between them they experimented with styles from realism to abstraction, yet each remained unique, powerfully inventive and often at the forefront of contemporary art.

Public art

In the early 1930s Moore joined a small group of avant-garde artists, along with his friend Hepworth, plus Gabo (see pp.44–5), Roland Penrose (1900–1984) and the art critic Herbert Read (1893–1968). In their frequent trips to Paris the group was in contact with leading progressive artists, notably Picasso, Braque, Arp and Giacometti. During the Second World War Moore was commissioned as a war artist, and after the War he began receiving important international commissions. These massive open-air sculptures were paid for by local or national governments to be put in public places in towns and cities. In 1977 he established the Henry Moore Foundation to promote the public appreciation of art and to preserve his sculptures.

Moore and Hepworth frequently bounced ideas off each other, using natural materials to produce smooth, undulating pieces that often appear as if they have always been in the landscape, either left by some primitive society or created by nature. Moore and Hepworth and her husband, artist Ben Nicholson (1894–1982), became key figures in the Modern Movement in Britain in the 1930s. Their circle became increasingly significant as European artists such as Gabo and Mondrian fled to London during the Second World War. Hepworth moved to Cornwall during the War, where she was prominent among the St Ives artists.

Symbolic spiders

Unlike Moore and Hepworth, Louise Bourgeois works on symbolising emotions. At 15 she studied mathematics at the Sorbonne in Paris – her studies of geometry contributed to her early Cubist drawings – and she worked as an assistant to Léger. In 1938 she moved to New York City, but her real success as an artist only came in the 1970s. Best known for her cells and spiders, she has worked in many different media and explores abstraction and symbolism. Her focus is often on relationships, sometimes conveying feelings of anger, betrayal and jealousy, but always with a sense of humour. In 1999 she created a nine-metre-high spider for Tate Modern in London. Called *Maman*, it symbolises a mother's strength, with its metaphors of spinning, weaving, nurture and protection.

MOORE, HEPWORTH & BOURGEOIS

*'All art should have a certain mystery
and should make demands on the spectator.'
Henry Moore*

HOLEY FIGURES

Moore and Hepworth worked with their surroundings, creating shapes and forms that were cunningly carved to become part of their landscape or background. Moore became known for his large-scale abstractions in cast bronze and carved marble and other stone, which are often of human figures with lumpy and hollow areas and – holes. He particularly liked creating reclining figures or mother and child sculptures, but why the holes? Well, because you can see through and round the forms; whether small or huge, they become part of the surroundings.

Opposite top Barbara Hepworth, *Forms in Echelon* 1938, polished teak wood, 108 x 60 x 71, Tate
Hepworth always liked putting her sculpture in the landscape and relating it to ancient art. These look like two monoliths: Hepworth said that the large stones put in place by people centuries ago are like giants striding across the landscape and she wanted to convey a similar feeling.

Opposite bottom Henry Moore, *Four-Piece Composition: Reclining Figure* 1934, Cumberland alabaster, 17.5 x 45.7 x 20.3, Tate
Carved in alabaster from fields in Cumbria, the bone- or stone-like shapes reflect Moore's interest in organic and mineral forms, and also echo both prehistoric stone carving and Picasso's work. The individual objects are abstract, but together, they resemble a reclining female body.

Louise Bourgeois, *Maman* 1999, steel and marble, 927.1 x 891.5 x 1023.6, Tate
Maman represents a female spider carrying her white marble eggs beneath her. Bourgeois said, 'The Spider is an ode to my mother. She was my best friend. Like a spider, my mother was a weaver ... Like spiders, my mother was very clever. Spiders are friendly presences that eat mosquitoes. We know that mosquitoes spread diseases and are therefore unwanted. So, spiders are helpful and protective, just like my mother.'

As the 20th century progressed, artists' thoughts about cities began to be less optimistic. Before the First World War, remember how the Futurists and others celebrated machines, urban development and speed? Well, that all changed. From 1914 to 1945 the economies of America and Europe were battered by two world wars and a depression. Artists, as ever, expressed their feelings and reflected the inadequacies of society in various ways.

Making a stir

Edward Hopper (1882–1967) was born in New York and studied illustration at the New York Institute of Art and Design. One of his teachers, artist Robert Henri (1865–1929), encouraged his students to use their art to 'make a stir in the world' and motivated students to render realistic depictions of urban life. Henri's students, many of whom developed into important artists, became known as the Ashcan School. Although Hopper visited Europe, he was unmoved by the Cubist and Fauvist works he saw, preferring the detail of the Realist painters. He was also fascinated by shadows on houses caused by turrets, porches and sloping roofs and his favourite thing was painting sunlight on the side of a house. He became known for painting scenes of urban life with strong atmospheres of loneliness, sadness and sometimes even menace. His work often seems as if we're looking in on other people's lives without them being aware of us, with each painting almost like a still from a film – giving us clues about the people, their actions and feelings and the bleak despondency of the era.

Nature-based abstractions

Georgia O'Keeffe (1887–1986) attended the Art Students League in New York City in 1907. She was later introduced to the ideas of Arthur Wesley Dow (1857–1922), who encouraged artists to express themselves through harmonious compositions and contrasts of light and dark. In 1916, a friend took some of her drawings to 291, the gallery owned by Alfred Stieglitz, who said that they were the 'purest, finest, sincerest things that had entered 291 in a long while.' Later that year he exhibited 10 of her drawings and in 1924, he and O'Keeffe were married. Through his circle, O'Keeffe met many early American Modernists. Soon after moving to New York she began making large-scale paintings of close-up natural forms, as if seen through a magnifying glass and during the 1920s she painted both natural and architectural forms, from large-scale flowers to New York skyscrapers. By the early 1930s she was spending time in New Mexico, exploring the colours and rugged scenery. Her nature-based abstractions show influences of Matisse, the photographers she mixed with and the writings of Kandinsky (see pp.34–5).

Edward Hopper, *House by the Railroad* 1925, oil on canvas, 61 x 73.7 , Museum of Modern Art, New York

Hopper derived his subject matter from the common features of American life, using sharp lines, large shapes and unusual lighting to capture lonely atmospheres. This painting of a solitary 19th-century house, standing alone against railway tracks, shows his understanding of the despair of many people at that time, with space, height and depth conveying a sense of loneliness.

HOPPER & O'KEEFFE

'No amount of skilful invention can replace the essential element of imagination.'
Edward Hopper

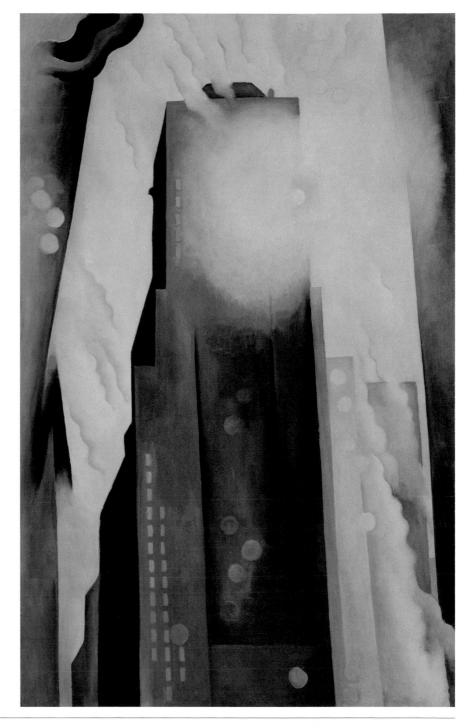

REMOVAL OF PRECONCEPTIONS

In the early 1900s, a growing
number of artists in America
challenged several conventions of
the past. Many wanted to replace
the moral restraints of society
with a new open-minded attitude.
Not quite as rigid as the French
academies of the 19th century,
the early 20th century, American
academies nevertheless wanted
artists to adhere to traditions that
integrated with what they believed
were the country's heritage and
values. Yet these modern American
artists preferred to embrace the
freedom on which their country
was founded.

**Georgia O'Keeffe, *The Shelton with
Sunspots* 1926, oil on canvas, 123.2 x 76.8,
The Art Institute of Chicago**
From the mid-1920s O'Keeffe began to
paint images of the city as she saw it: she
and her husband Alfred Stieglitz rented
an apartment on the 28th floor of the
hotel shown here. Between 1926 and
1929 she produced several paintings
of New York skyscrapers as symbols
of the modern world. These works are
atmospheric and powerful with strong
lines and shapes and lighting derived
from photography. But in contrast to
Hopper's work, O'Keeffe's image seems
optimistic; the evolving modern city a
vision of hope for the future.

The ideas of the Bauhaus were not for everyone. As a result of the social tensions leading up to the Second World War, several German artists preferred criticising and making satirical visual comments about the developments in their country, to constructing clean lines and balanced designs.

A world gone mad

This movement became called the New Objectivity or Neue Sachlichkeit after an exhibition held in 1923, and it essentially ended in 1933 when the Nazis rose to power. The movement was different from the Bauhaus and Expressionism, both of which developed in Germany: although the artists' styles varied, they all shared a detached and objective approach to their subjects. Leading lights among them were Otto Dix (1891–1969) and George Grosz (1893–1959) who were horrified at the way events were unfolding in their country. Both men had served in the First World War where they experienced atrocious conditions in the trenches and they violently opposed the way that things now seemed to be developing. The political and economic situation in Germany during the 1920s and 1930s was extremely unstable. The poor became poorer while the rich flaunted their wealth and power. Both Dix and Grosz had been Dadaists (see pp.46–7), and this method of painting allowed them to convey their aversion to the current situation. Dix expressed his disgust through bitter depictions of the carnage of war and the corruption of the wealthy inhabitants of his home town, Berlin. Grosz hated authority – indeed, he was nearly shot for insubordination during the First World War. After a nervous breakdown in 1917 he was declared unfit for service, so he spent the rest of his life drawing and painting images reflecting his horror of warfare and his disillusionment and revulsion for German society. Dix said that his paintings were visions of 'mankind gone mad'. His work encouraged other artists to consider the implications of wars and the societies that instigated them.

ART IN CONTEXT

RELIGIOUS REFERENCES

Many of the Neue Sachlichkeit artists made references to the Bible, often painting in styles similar to historical painters who produced religious art or using sacred symbolism in a cynical manner.

NEW OBJECTIVITY

'Painting is the effort to produce order; order in yourself. There is much chaos in me, much chaos in our time.'
Otto Dix

Opposite **George Grosz, *Suicide* 1916, oil on canvas, 100 x 77.5, Tate**
Experiences in the German Army left Grosz deeply shocked, and with an intense loathing for society. After discharge from the army, he produced mercilessly mocking paintings and drawings that 'expressed my despair, hate and disillusionment'. This distorted, angular view of a Berlin street was painted during the First World War. Dogs roam past the bodies of people who have committed suicide, while a prostitute blatantly shows off to an old man. Grosz uses red to express anger and pain, revealing his disgust at the lack of morals in Germany at that time.

Otto Dix, *War Triptych* 1929–32, tempera on wood, overall dimensions 306 x 408, Gemäldegalerie Neue Meister, Dresden
This work is composed in the same way as the great German painter Matthias Grünewald (c.1470–1528) created traditional religious scenes in an intense and expressive style. In Dix's triptych, however, the central panel shows a ghastly vision where a soldier, his face covered by a gas mask, is left the sole survivor in a collapsed trench. Corpses decompose all around, while a skeleton hangs from a tree. Dix has depicted himself rescuing another soldier in the right-hand panel. In the foreground, the bodies of men lie under tent canvases.

By the late 1930s the First World War had been over for twenty years, but the intervening years had been grim, what with the loss of millions of young men's lives and with worldwide economic problems. Modern artists often commented on the politics of the day, but rarely did they get into trouble for it. Well, not serious trouble anyway. All that changed when the Nazi party rose to power in Germany. Dictators in general do not like abstract art as it doesn't glorify what they do. Meanwhile, they use artistic propaganda to tell the public what they should believe in.

Art and power

Hitler, Mussolini and other dictators of the world war years forced artists to produce what they believed was pure art that would promote their ideas. Tolerance of artists varied from country to country. Italian artists favoured by the Fascist regime of Mussolini included major figures of the 1930s, such as the sculptor Arturo Martini (1889–1947) and the painter Mario Sironi (1885–1961). In Germany the situation was extreme and art that the Nazis labelled 'degenerate' (see pp.36–7) was confiscated or destroyed. They seized over 20,000 works by more than 200 artists. Earlier in his life Hitler had failed as an artist, so he was resentful of others.

ART & POLITICS

'It is my duty to voice the suffering of men, the never-ending sufferings heaped mountain-high.'
Käthe Kollwitz

Left Max Beckmann, *Carnival* 1920, oil on canvas, 186.4 x 91.8, Tate
Beckmann's work, with its grotesque and distorted figures, characterised what the Nazis considered degenerate art, and in 1933 he was dismissed from his teaching post in Frankfurt. Several of his works were included in the 1937 *Entartete Kunst* exhibition, prompting him to leave Germany for Amsterdam. This painting represents a carnival, with fancy dress and a clown. The two figures were based on close friends of Beckmann, while he himself is probably the masked clown, expressing the underlying emotions of events that surrounded him.

He was not interested in artists and viewers examining emotions or social problems, but instead wanted paintings to show a happy world populated by blue-eyed, golden-haired, white-skinned people. Dix, Beckmann, Nolde, Kandinsky, Munch, Klee, Kollwitz and Picasso were all labelled degenerate, while other artists who conformed to Hitler's ideal were promoted by the Nazis.

In 1937 in Munich the Nazis held an art exhibition called *Entartete Kunst* (*Degenerate Art*) with the aim of showing the German public what art was not acceptable, and to proclaim the 'degenerate' artists as mad. Works of art were crammed together, with mocking labels. People flocked in their thousands to the exhibition, and when it closed the art was sold, raising more money for the Nazis. They were good psychologists: by humiliating the artists, they didn't create martyrs, but made them look foolish in the eyes of society.

Pablo Picasso, *Guernica* 1937, oil on canvas, 349.3 x 776.6, Museo Reina Sofia, Madrid

Picasso remained in Paris during the Spanish Civil War and the Second World War. He painted *Guernica* as a bitter attack on the Spanish Fascist government, even though it had been commissioned by representatives of the Spanish Republic and he didn't want it shown in Spain until General Franco was either dead or deposed. Picasso died in 1973 and Franco died in 1975. In 1981, the painting arrived in Spain, where it remains to this day. Away from the oppression of Fascist governments Picasso was able to express his horror freely. If this had been painted with realistic figures, it would not be so horrific or shocking. He used only black, grey and white to reinforce the sombre despair of the subject and included distorted victims of the bombed town. A woman screams from a burning building; a mother wails over her dead baby; a horse neighs in agony and a mutilated soldier holds a broken sword in one hand. Try to work out what other objects and figures in the painting might represent. Picasso said: 'The horse represents the people and the bull brutality and darkness.'

Abstract Expressionism grew out of Surrealism just after the Second World War. There were two groups: Action painters and Colour Field painters. All of them were preoccupied with the paint and the process of painting, rather than the subject.

ART IN CONTEXT

BUT IS IT ART?

People love to criticise Action painting. It can look messy and some artists' claims were rather pretentious. So next time someone says 'Call that art?' or 'You having a laugh?', tell them this:

- Most of the artists were searching for something beyond appearances.
- None of the works pretends to be anything other than a painting.
- The rhythms and colours should be enjoyed for what they are, just as music is enjoyed for itself.
- Stare at some of these works, quietly and without distractions, you will begin to feel tranquil or uplifted.

But even though the artists made their work look as if it was produced involuntarily, most of it was carefully planned. Jackson Pollock's large works were created by spattering, flicking, dripping and sloshing paint on huge canvases placed on the floor, earning him the nickname 'Jack the Dripper'. He moved about as he worked, immersing himself in the action of painting and expressing his deepest thoughts. He said that there was no accident in the result of his work. Other Abstract Expressionists include Willem de Kooning (1904–97), Ad Reinhardt (1913–67), Philip Guston (1913–80) and Robert Motherwell (1915–91).

ABSTRACT EXPRESSIONISM

'The modern artist is working with space and time, and expressing his feelings rather than illustrating.'
Jackson Pollock

Big drip

In the mid-1940s, Abstract Expressionism emerged in New York City and became prominent over the following decade. It was the first major American movement to:

- involve a fairly large number of artists,
- be independent from European styles and
- influence the development of art abroad.

Abstract Expressionists began working in this way, they said, in response to the horror of the Nuclear Age. The style also developed from European Surrealist Automatism (see pp. 66–7). Unconcerned with representing the physical world, artists aimed to express their own and to inspire others' emotions through paint. They painted freely, often with large brushes, sometimes dripping or even throwing paint onto their huge canvases. The action of producing the painting was as important as the work itself. Concentration on the brushstrokes and the physical action of painting made Abstract Expressionism different from many other modern art movements, but in appearance some of the results resemble works by J.M.W. Turner (1775–1851) or some of Monet's later paintings.

Fields of colour

Other Abstract Expressionists saturated their canvases with large expanses of intense, often flat, single colour, blurred at the edges and with no frames or boundaries. Colour Field artists eliminated the emotional, personal and gestural application of the other Abstract Expressionists, although their work is meant to make viewers feel calm or uplifted. Mark Rothko (1903–70) and Barnett Newman (1905–70) are examples of Colour Field artists.

Opposite Arshile Gorky, *Waterfall* **1943,
oil on canvas, 153.7 x 113, Tate**
Gorky (1904–48) settled in the US in 1920.
His use of free-flowing colour and line
were inspired by Surrealism and nature:
here, formless shapes and drips of fluid
paint suggest the flow of a waterfall seen
through trees.

Top Jackson Pollock, *Yellow Islands* **1952,
oil on canvas, 143.5 x 185.4, Tate**
Pollock aimed to express himself directly
through the paint. He began by pouring
black paint onto the canvas, adding
yellow and crimson on top with a brush.
He then lifted the canvas upright while
the paint was still wet, allowing it to run.

Bottom Mark Rothko, *Black on Maroon*
1958, oil on canvas, 266.5 x 366, Tate
Rothko's aim was to create in viewers
a feeling of peace. This is one of the
paintings he produced as part of a
commission for the Four Seasons
Restaurant in New York. He wanted to
create a reflective atmosphere, but in
the end he gave the paintings to Tate
because he felt that a restaurant was the
wrong place for his work.

The fact that Abstract Expressionism deliberately avoided reflecting the outside world made it hard for the public to understand. In 1960, partly as a reaction against the movement, some artists set out to rebuild the link between art and life. The French art critic Pierre Restany (1930–2003) wrote a manifesto for Nouveau Réalisme, or New Realism, which was signed by nine artists including Yves Klein (1928–62), Daniel Spoerri (born 1930) and Jean Tinguely (1925–91). Several others also joined the group over the next couple of years. The new movement was called 'New Realism' not because the artists wanted to paint realistically in the traditional sense, but because they wanted to explore the modern life and consumer culture that had been developing rapidly since the end of the Second World War, and because they used real objects in their work.

New Realism was compared to Pop art, which emerged during the 1950s and 1960s, but the diverse ideas of the New Realists were closer to Dadaism than Pop.

Discarded objects

Just as the Dadaists had done, and Duchamp in particular, the New Realists painted and produced collages using discarded objects. German artist Wolf Vostell (1932–98) believed that destruction was everywhere, and he developed what he called 'décollage', or torn poster technique, making works from accumulated layers of posters from advertising hoardings. By presenting these concoctions of objects that no one else wanted as art, these artists were questioning how things were produced and used by post-war society.

It's a wrap!

Christo and Jeanne-Claude (both born 13th June 1935) use fabric to create ephemeral works of art in urban and rural sites (see pp.90–91). Taking over entire environments, their temporary works encourage viewers to perceive locations with fresh eyes and a new awareness of the surroundings. Many of their works involve vast expanses of fabric, suspended or arranged in the environment to make viewers see entire locations with fresh perspectives.

ROLY-POLY PAINTINGS

Yves Klein was enormously inventive in his short career, using his and other people's bodies to create art. (They agreed to it first.) He invented his own deep blue paint, called 'International Klein Blue' or IKB. On several occasions he created paintings which he called *Anthropometries* in front of an audience at a gallery. While an orchestra played his one-chord *Monotone Symphony*, Klein, dressed in a tuxedo and white gloves, directed models covered with IKB paint to twist, press or roll over canvas or paper. Once they had created the desired effect, he told them to get off (see p.94).

NEW REALISM

'To me art is a form of manifest revolt, total and complete'
Jean Tinguely

Opposite **Yves Klein,** *IKB 79* **1959, paint on canvas on wood, 139.7 x 119.7 x 32, Tate**
In 1947 Klein began making monochrome paintings, keeping them free from personal expression or representation. Ten years later, he developed and patented his trademark colour, IKB, and for him, this intense blue represented infinity (remember Marc and Kandinsky's belief in the spiritual aspects of the colour blue – p.35). Klein described his colour as 'Blue in itself, disengaged from all functional justification' and he made around 200 paintings with it. He didn't give titles to the works, but after his death his widow assigned a number to each one.

Daniel Spoerri, *Prose Poems* **1959–60, mixed media relief on wood, 69 x 54.2 x 36.1, Tate**
Spoerri called his relief works 'tableaux-pièges' (picture-traps) because they involved fixing objects in random positions on table tops or in drawers. They were hung vertically on walls and were intended to make viewers feel uncomfortable because they're not what usually hangs in art galleries. Here, the remains of a meal are preserved on a wooden board that Spoerri used as a table while he was living in a small room in a Paris hotel. The title comes from the book in the corner by the poet, Robert Walser.

During the 1950s in Europe and North America, after the austerity of the Second World War there was a boom in mass-produced goods and mass entertainment which became known as popular – or pop – culture. It inspired an art movement in England and America which became known as Pop art.

Pop artists wanted to brighten up the world that had been damaged by two world wars and to celebrate modern life. In some ways, they were critical of society and any art that was difficult to understand. The idea that art is only for a few people who understand it – usually the rich and privileged – has often irritated modern artists, and Pop artists in particular tried to make art that was as accessible as fast food, television and pop music.

THE SWINGING SIXTIES

From miniskirts to J.F. Kennedy and the Beatles, the 1960s had plenty to swing about. An advertising copywriter coined the name 'teenager', and for the first time young people had their own identity and didn't have to model themselves on their parents. Not everything was good, but the new ideas about life, fashion, music, architecture, design and art gave the decade a refreshing and individual style. Pop art celebrated this.

Let it be…

In 1957 Richard Hamilton, one of the leading Pop artists, summed up eleven things that he thought Pop art should be:

Popular	Young
Transient	Witty
Expendable	Sexy
Low-cost	Gimmicky
Mass-produced	Glamorous
Big business	

Art for everybody

The term 'Pop art' was first used in 1958 by the English critic Lawrence Alloway (1926–90) to describe art that was created from images of popular culture and society. Artists who had grown up during the Second World War were now witnessing the marketing of new products. They based their work on images that everyone could relate to – advertising, slogans and the media, or just bold, flat arrangements of colour. Whether working in two or three dimensions, they used methods from mass-produced commercial art, such as screen-printing. Pop artists working in Britain included Richard Hamilton (born 1922), Eduardo Paolozzi (1924–2005), Peter Blake (born 1932) and David Hockney (born 1937), and in America, Andy Warhol (1928–87), Jasper Johns (born 1930), Robert Rauschenberg (1925–2008) and Roy Lichtenstein (1923–97).

Many people questioned whether Pop art was 'real' art at all: it commented, often humorously, on Western society; nobody needed specialist knowledge to understand it; and it blurred the distinction between commercial and fine art. Never before had painting and sculpture been so close to what was going on in the rest of society. Yet at the time it put the art establishment's nose out of joint.

Optimistic spirit

Pop art reflected the light-hearted attitudes that people craved after the Second World War. It was also a descendant of Dada and a reaction against Abstract Expressionism. But unlike Dada, it wasn't an angry reaction against contemporary society; and like Abstract Expressionism, it was always about real things in society. It developed as an expression of hope for the future.

POP ART

'During the 1960s, I think, people forgot what emotions were supposed to be. And I don't think they've ever remembered.'
Andy Warhol

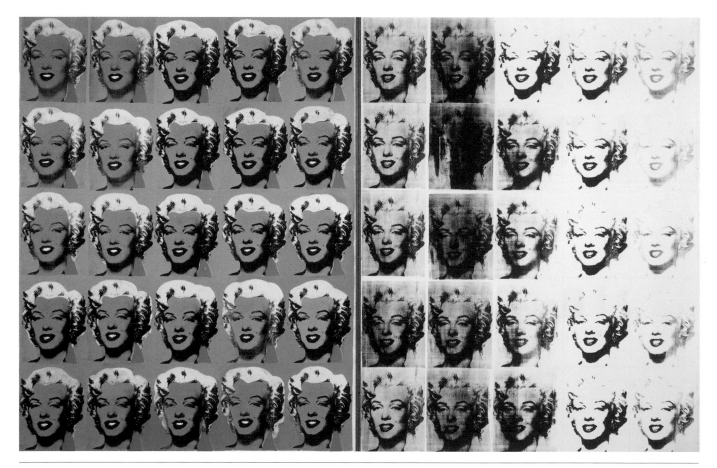

Opposite Richard Hamilton, *Swingeing London* **1967, acrylic, emulsion, silkscreen, ink and collage on canvas, 67.3 x 85.1, Tate**
In 1967 the Rolling Stones' Mick Jagger and Keith Richards, along with Hamilton's art dealer Robert Fraser, were arrested for possession of illegal drugs. Hamilton commemorated this with prints, paintings and a poster taken from a photograph of Jagger and Richards in the back of a car, covering their faces from the paparazzi. The title is a pun on the 'Swinging Sixties', when the behaviour of some was 'swingeing' (excessive).

Andy Warhol, *Marilyn Diptych* **1962, acrylic on canvas, 205.4 x 144.8 x 20, Tate**
This is one of the many paintings and prints that Warhol produced of Marilyn Monroe just after she died in 1962, highlighting the public's obsession with celebrity. He chose a publicity photo from 1953, cropped it to emphasise Marilyn's face, and then printed it on several canvases using the silkscreen process.

Before we go any further, remember that Pop artists didn't try to make their art clever. You can't look at it and say 'Wow! What skill and talent!' They didn't aim for that reaction, but quite the opposite. Talking of opposites, the diversity of Pop art can be summed up in the work of two artists who were so different from each other that one could be forgiven for thinking they belonged to different art movements.

Jasper Johns

One of the chief artists to move American art away from Abstract Expressionism was Jasper Johns. He met and became a close friend of fellow artist Rauschenberg, and influenced others in both Pop and Op art. The story goes that when he was about 25 the idea of painting the American flag came to him in a dream. He destroyed all his previous work and began producing a series of paintings of things like targets, maps, flags, letters and numbers. These works certainly did not come from his subconscious, but were copies of objects from popular culture. His paintings are about as familiar as any object can be yet, far from being simple, they are full of meanings about being an American in the 20th century.

He wanted to move art away from its reliance on the emotions and to paint objectively. He liked to exaggerate the surfaces he was working on, making thick relief shapes to help describe his images. He often used encaustic (wax-based paint) and plaster relief to give extra texture to his paintings; he also produced bronze sculptures. By the 1960s his work had become more untidy and more subjective, and more mocking of the Abstract Expressionists.

LEGACY

Both Johns and Warhol were inspired by Duchamp and Picabia's rejection of artistic conventions, in particular by Duchamp's concept of the readymade and Picabia's use of popular imagery in his paintings.

JOHNS & WARHOL

'Everyone is of course free to interpret the work in his own way. I think seeing a picture is one thing and interpreting it is another.'
Jasper Johns

Andy Warhol

Death, consumerism and fame fascinated Warhol throughout his life. Most people know of his prediction that one day everyone would have 15 minutes of fame. His obsession with fame developed as his outlook was shaped by the mass media: by multiplying images of familiar, famous faces (see p.81) Warhol demonstrated the effects of media repetition, showing how replication dulls the senses and makes things seem commonplace. The consumer boom of the 1950s in America and then in Europe was given momentum by easy credit, consumer television and the post-War 'baby boom'. As Warhol saw, ordinary items could develop iconic status.

Horrified by the notion of death, his work often dwelt on catastrophes such as car crashes and accidental poisonings. In the same way as he reduced celebrities and consumer products to impersonal and mundane objects, he also took away the shock value of tragedies by repeating images over and again.

Opposite **Jasper Johns, *Target with Four Faces* 1955, encaustic on newspaper and cloth over canvas surmounted by four tinted-plaster faces in wood box with hinged front, 85.3 x 66 x 7.6, Museum of Modern Art, New York**

In the 1950s Johns began to base his paintings on ordinary, familiar objects that were also symbolic of the American society he was part of. He painted things he called 'what the mind already knows.' Mixing thick paint, wax encaustic and collage, he gave extra texture to simple images, like this target. The result is an abstract image, but one that can be uncovered to reveal objects from the real world.

Andy Warhol, *Black Bean*, from *Soup Can Series I* 1968, screenprint on paper, 89.2 x 59.1, Tate

Familiar consumer items such as Coca-Cola bottles and soup cans became a regular subject for Warhol during the 1960s. Painting or printing everyday objects as works of art was Warhol's way of mocking the snobbery of the art world and scoffing at consumerism. Using screenprinting he imitated the machine-produced designs of the objects, reminding viewers that he is using commercial techniques to produce art. Here he also questions how we value and view art: the actual print is a consumer object masquerading as 'high art'.

Some art creates the illusion of movement, even if the work doesn't actually move. In 1964 an exhibition was held in the Museum of Modern Art in New York, displaying works that seemed to quiver and whirl on the walls. An article in *Time Magazine* named the movement 'Op art', short for 'Optical art'.

Visual vitality

The New York exhibition was called *The Responsive Eye* and included works by artists such as Frank Stella (born 1936), Alexander Liberman (1912–99), Victor Vasarely (1908–97) and Bridget Riley. Other prominent Op artists included Jesus Rafael Soto (1923–2005) and Richard Anuszkiewicz (born 1930). The artists didn't work closely together or write a manifesto, but their work emerged at the same time in different places. Vasarely had worked as a poster designer in Paris, but from the 1960s he applied simple visual tricks that he had learned in his advertising work to his artwork, including ways of making lines and shapes on flat canvases appear to look small, large, hollow, spherical or even throbbing. He was interested in a form of art that everyone could understand, not just those with particular educational backgrounds and experiences. Riley originally worked in a restricted palette of black and white, using shapes and lines that work with our eyes and create the effect of colours and movement. (Remember Delaunay, pp.42–3? He also explored the way our eyes work, but with a different approach.)

Critics dismissed Op art as visual trickery, but when you think about it the illusion of perspective that artists have been using for centuries to make images on flat surfaces appear three-dimensional is very similar. Still, Op art became increasingly popular and, to Riley's annoyance, images were used in packaging and designs of the Swinging Sixties. She even tried to sue an American company, without success, for using one of her paintings as the basis of a fabric design.

HARD EDGE

Another art movement that had links with Op art and Colour Field (see pp.76–7), as well as with Mondrian (see pp.13 and 52–3), was Hard Edge painting. In their reaction to the gestural forms of Abstract Expressionism, Hard Edge artists produced work devoid of personal feeling. They painted canvases in areas of solid colour with precise, straight (or hard) edges. Vasarely, Riley, Stella and Liberman were associated with Hard Edge painting, along with Barnett Newman, Ellsworth Kelly (born 1923) and Ad Reinhardt (see pp.76–7).

OP ART

'For me nature is not landscape, but the dynamism of visual forces.'
Bridget Riley

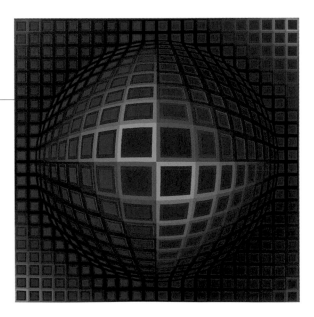

for Christopher Prater - '64
Bridget Riley.

Artist's Proof

Opposite Victor Vasarely, *Vega-Nor* 1969, oil on canvas, 200 x 200, Albright-Knox Art Gallery, New York
This painting creates the illusion of a sphere on a flat surface, thanks to Vasarely's use of colour, shape and line. Warm colours appear to come forward (see pp.16–17), and are applied here around the central squares, making them seem to pop out. The largest and least distorted shapes are also in the centre. Shapes become narrower and smaller away from the centre, which makes them seem to recede. The lines – some straight, some curved – are also carefully calculated to strengthen the illusion.

Bridget Riley, *Blaze* 1964, screenprint on paper, 53 x 52.1, Tate
Like Vasarely, Riley also worked in advertising before becoming absorbed by creating optical effects. This screenprint seems to spin and zigzag before your eyes, colours shimmering between the black lines. At the same time it has the effect of a tunnel, disappearing towards the hole in the centre – or is it the centre? By playing with our eyes, Riley achieved more than just a two-dimensional illusion.

You will by now have realised that a lot of creative ideas originate from the same starting place, but turn out differently. Three completely different artists who worked during the same period, exploring ideas, using influences and influencing others in turn, are: Joseph Beuys (1921–86), Anthony Caro (born 1924) and Cy Twombly (born 1928). Like other modern artists, all three investigated new materials and ways of working. By the 1960s they had expanded their range beyond the traditional materials of paint, bronze and marble. Technique and skills had been so important in the past, but now the idea behind the work took precedence.

Marvellous materials

Beuys was a German artist who became most famous for his public performances and his belief in the healing potential of art. He also produced sculptures, prints, posters and drawings. A charismatic and controversial figure, he produced watercolours and drawings showing his interest in Christianity, mythology, botany and zoology. In 1962 he became briefly involved with Fluxus, an international network of artists, composers and designers who combined different artistic materials and disciplines (see pp.94–5), but then became more interested in Performance art. He also focused on both the symbolic and physical properties of the materials he used: for example, he used fur, felt and animal fat to explore ideas of warmth, insulation and protection.

Metal guru

Caro is a British abstract sculptor whose metal constructions are often made of 'found' industrial objects. He gained a degree in engineering and spent time in the Royal Navy before studying sculpture. In the 1950s he worked as an assistant to Henry Moore, and within ten years he had abandoned his figurative approach and started welding or bolting together bronze, steel and aluminium. He often painted finished pieces in bold, flat colours. He inspired a younger generation of abstract sculptors, including Richard Long (born 1945) and Gilbert & George (born 1943 and 1942 respectively). Caro's sculptures usually stand directly on the floor, removing a barrier between the work and the viewer.

BEUYS, CARO & TWOMBLY

'How you respond to a sculpture, how a viewer sees the sculpture, is vital.'
Anthony Caro

Anthony Caro, *The Soldier's Tale* 1983, painted steel, approx.183 x 208 x 134.5, Tate
Early in the 1980s Caro began using scrap metal from marine dockyards. Here he has cut and arranged sheets of steel to produce a frame and inserted a large cup-like form that looks rather like a mouth singing. The title refers to a piece of music by Igor Stravinsky (1882–1971). Caro said that just as musical notes combine into a melody, so individual parts of his sculpture fit together in harmony. (How many other artists have made musical connections?)

On your marks

Cy Twombly is an American Abstract Expressionist, known for his large, scribbled, graffiti-style paintings on predominantly grey, fawn or beige backgrounds. By the 1960s he had stopped representing recognisable subjects, saying that marks such as lines or smudges were themselves the subjects of his work. Sometimes his marks are obscure, at other times they are clear, but they are nearly always symbolic. In the mid-1970s Twombly began to suggest landscapes with colour, adding written inscriptions and collage; his later landscapes have become even freer and more abstract.

Cy Twombly, *Primavera*, from *Quattro Stagioni (A Painting in Four Parts)* 1993–5, acrylic, oil, crayon and pencil on canvas, 313.2 x 189.5, Tate
Twombly produced four different paintings in this series, using a range of colours to indicate the changing light and temperatures of the seasons. This work, representing spring, describes a renewal after winter in a vertical arrangement of red curves and splashes of yellow. The Italian word for spring, 'primavera', appears next to descriptions of happiness and hope.

Joseph Beuys, *Felt Suit* 1970, felt, approx. 170 x 60, Tate
As one of Beuys' own suits, this is a type of self-portrait. Although it was intended as a work to be hung from the gallery wall, he also wore it in an art performance in the early 1970s. He said that the suit was an extension of his felt sculptures, in which the felt appeared as 'an element of warmth'.

Less is more, so some say, and if your friends think the modern art we've considered so far is easy to criticise, then tell them to look away now as Minimalism looks as if it's about nothing much at all. But, as by now you will have gathered, there is always a point or purpose and always something in contemporary society that triggers creative ideas.

PUBLIC OUTRAGE

Minimalism, perhaps above all art movements, caused uproar among the public and the press. The critics had a field day, but:

- Minimalism was not intended to be compared with traditional art, in the way it was produced or in the way it was meant to be considered.
- Its aim was to allow viewers to consider objects without further distractions, such as composition, subject or technique.
- The artists didn't say they were producing anything original, just asking viewers to think differently.

MINIMALISM

'My art springs from my desire to have things in the world which would otherwise never be there.'
Carl Andre

Bare essentials

As people grew tired of the psychedelic Sixties and Abstract Expressionism, in the USA in the second half of the 1960s, Minimalism began to emerge. The term 'minimalist' is often applied to anything that is stripped to its fundamental elements, but the art movement has links with other movements such as Conceptual art, where finished work exists merely to convey a theory, with Pop art's interest in the impersonal, and with the simple constructions of Land art. Minimalism also took on the Constructivist idea that art should be made of modern, industrial materials. Reducing work to its essentials and creating simple geometric shapes, usually in three-dimensions, Minimalist work is always devoid of personal expression and is never an imitation of something else. Minimalist artists include Donald Judd, Carl Andre, Richard Serra (born 1939), Dan Flavin (1933–96) and Ellsworth Kelly.

The bricks

Carl Andre was influenced by Brancusi (see p.10 and pp.26–7) and his friend Frank Stella. In the 1960s he began constructing works from simple blocks of various materials, often using standard industrial units such as bricks or metal plates. In the late 1960s he made eight sculptures using building bricks, one of which was bought by Tate in 1972. During an exhibition of the work in 1976 the press and public couldn't contain themselves, with jeers of 'Call that art?' and 'What a load of rubbish!'

Ladders and lights

Judd and Flavin also specialised in repeating one shape or form in different works. Judd often constructed wall-mounted 'ladders' or boxes, while Flavin put fluorescent lights where you'd least expect them: in corners, on the floor and around windows and doors. The reflected light and shadows appear to make some areas disappear. He called his art 'situational' as, like other Minimalists, he didn't consider his work permanent. Serra, meanwhile, is interested in the process of making his art and in how viewers interpret it in their own individual ways.

Opposite top **Donald Judd, *Untitled* 1980, steel, aluminium and Perspex, 22.9 x 101.6 x 78.7, Tate**
One of the most significant American artists of the post-war period, Donald Judd changed the course of modern sculpture. Most of his 'stacks' or 'ladders' consist of ten elements, each placed with strictly measured distances between them: the gaps between each element and between the first element and the floor were equal to the height of a single element. There is nothing more going on: Judd's work is simply about shapes, proportions and spaces around each structure. You either get it, or you don't.

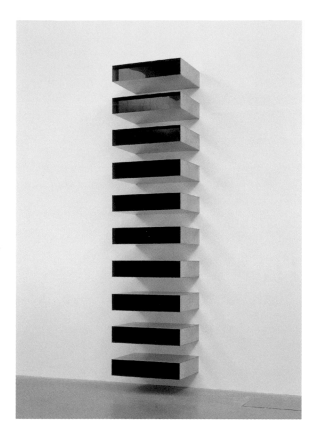

Carl Andre, *Equivalent VIII* 1966, firebricks, 12.7 x 68.6 x 229.2, Tate
Although Andre's eight *Equivalent* sculptures are made out of arrangements of 120 firebricks, his inspiration came from water. Each arrangement is different, but they all have the same height, mass and volume and are therefore 'equivalent' to each other. Andre wanted viewers to consider the way they look at things, especially objects that have been designed for another job, when placed in mathematical order.

If people thought Duchamp's urinal was potty (see pp.48–9), they would have struggled even more with Conceptualism, which arose from Duchamp's original idea. In the mid-1960s, in both America and Europe, several artists began to exhibit conceptions in the form of drawings, texts or photos for works intended to encourage viewers to participate intellectually in the creative process.

The big idea

Conceptualists worked on the notion that ideas can be more important than actual works of art. They rebelled against the opinion that art is precious, and aimed to stop people from being passive when viewing it. In 1967, after journalist and artist Sol LeWitt (1928–2007) used the term 'Conceptualist' to define it, the art movement gained public recognition. The purpose of Conceptual art was merely to communicate ideas or record events and to put forward new ideas for viewers to consider. In order to minimise the importance of the creator and of traditional art forms such as painting and sculpture, conventional painting materials were rejected. Instead, film, writing, photographs, tapes, maps and other media not usually associated with art were used.

Supporters of Conceptualism believe that it expands the limits of art, while critics see it as dull and pretentious. Although some Conceptual artists attempted to make serious political and social statements, more often than not they were preoccupied with analysing the nature of art, believing that it is more important to convey a message than to worry about aesthetic factors. Many traditional art lovers understandably found this type of art difficult to appreciate, so Conceptual art never gained widespread popularity.

Meanings

Conceptual artists think beyond the limits of traditional media and work out their ideas in whatever materials and forms are appropriate. One of the recurring ideas is how to convey meaning, and words and sounds have therefore often been used. Joseph Kosuth (born 1945) uses language both as the material and the subject of his art: many of his works feature dictionary definitions. Conceptual artists include Beuys (see pp.86–7), Victor Burgin (born 1941), Michael Craig-Martin (born 1941), Gilbert & George, Yves Klein and Joseph Kosuth.

'ANYONE CAN DO IT'

Yes, that's right – anyone can do Conceptual art. That was many artists' point. Skill and dexterity were out. Conceptual art, like some other post-war movements, often required little or no physical craftsmanship, while traditional art is distinguished by requiring physical skill. For instance, many of LeWitt's works may be constructed by anyone simply by following a set of written instructions, while Roman Opalka (born 1931) simply painted numbers from one to infinity.

CONCEPTUALISM

'It's extraordinary stuff – what an artist has to do. You finish a big group of works, then the next day you have to begin again. Forty years we've been doing that.'
Gilbert

Q: To begin with, could you describe this work?
A: Yes, of course. What I've done is change a glass of water into a full-grown oak tree without altering the accidents of the glass of water.
Q: The accidents?
A: Yes. The colour, feel, weight, size …
Q: Do you mean that the glass of water is a symbol of an oak tree?
A: No. It's not a symbol. I've changed the physical substance of the glass of water into that of an oak tree.
Q: It looks like a glass of water …
A: Of course it does. I didn't change its appearance. But it's not a glass of water. It's an oak tree.
Q: Can you prove what you claim to have done?
A: Well, yes and no. I claim to have maintained the physical form of the glass of water and, as you can see, I have. However, as one normally looks for evidence of physical change in terms of altered form, no such proof exists.
Q: Haven't you simply called this glass of water an oak tree?
A: Absolutely not. It is not a glass of water any more. I have changed its actual substance. It would no longer be accurate to call it a glass of water. One could call it anything one wished but that would not alter the fact that it is an oak tree.
Q: Isn't this just a case of the emperor's new clothes?
A: No. With the emperor's new clothes people claimed to see something which wasn't there because they felt they should. I would be very surprised if anyone told me they saw an oak tree.
Q: Was it difficult to effect the change?
A: No effort at all. But it took me years of work before I realized I could do it.
Q: When precisely did the glass of water become an oak tree?
A: When I put water in the glass.
Q: Does this happen every time you fill a glass with water?
A: No, of course not. Only when I intend to change it into an oak tree.

Q: Then intention causes the change?
A: I would say it precipitates the change.
Q: You don't know how you do it?
A: It contradicts what I feel I know about cause and effect.
Q: It seems to me you're claiming to have worked a miracle. Isn't that the case?
A: I'm flattered that you think so.
Q: But aren't you the only person who can do something like this?
A: How could I know?
Q: Could you teach others to do it?
A: No. It's not something one can teach.
Q: Do you consider that changing the glass of water into an oak tree constitutes an artwork?
A: Yes.
Q: What precisely is the artwork? The glass of water?
A: There is no glass of water any more.
Q: The process of change?
A: There is no process involved in the change.
Q: The oak tree?
A: Yes. the oak tree.
Q: But the oak tree only exists in the mind.
A: No. The actual oak tree is physically present but in the form of the glass of water. As the glass of water was a particular glass of water, the oak tree is also particular. To conceive the category 'oak tree' or to picture a particular oak tree is not to understand and experience what appears to be a glass of water as an oak tree. Just as it is imperceivable, it is also inconceivable.
Q: Did the particular oak tree exist somewhere else before it took the form of the glass of water?
A: No. This particular oak tree did not exist previously. I should also point out that it does not and will not ever have any other form but that of a glass of water.
Q: How long will it continue to be an oak tree?
A: Until I change it.

Opposite **Christo and Jeanne-Claude,**
Running Fence, 1972–6, nylon, steel posts and cables, 5.5 m x 39.4 km, Sonoma and Marin Counties, California
Christo and Jeanne-Claude may be fitted into several art movements. They are often classed as Performance artists because the process is as important to them as the finished product. They are also Environmental artists and they are Conceptualists as their work always stems from a big idea. In 1972, they began preparations for this work to run through the Californian landscape to the sea. It was completed in 1976.

Top left and right **Michael Craig-Martin,**
An Oak Tree 1973, glass, water, shelf and printed text, variable dimensions, Tate; lent from a private collection
Hands down if you think this is a glass of water on a shelf. Wrong! The artist, Michael Craig-Martin asserts that it is actually an oak tree. In the text on the wall below, he discusses our understanding of art and our beliefs in the power of the artist. He is showing viewers that our perception of art changes depending on how the artist exhibits it.

Bottom **Joseph Kosuth,** *Clock (One and Five), English/Latin Version* 1965, clock, photograph and printed texts, 61 x 290.2, Tate
Investigations and representation have occupied Kosuth since 1965. Concerned with different forms of representation, this work brings together a real object with depictions of aspects of that object – in this case, a working clock, a photograph of it and enlarged entries from an English/Latin dictionary describing the words 'time', 'machination' and 'object'. At the time Kosuth was enthusiastic about the effects of language on the way we see and portray the world.

In the late 1960s some artists in the USA and Europe expanded the field of art quite literally and began making huge sculptures from natural materials, often in landscape settings. This became known as Land art or earthworks, and included the work of artists Richard Long, Robert Smithson (1938–73), Andy Goldsworthy (born 1956), Michael Heizer (born 1944) and others. Using stones, earth, sand, water and plants as raw materials they created works of art both in galleries and – more often – in the open air.

The great outdoors

Most of the work was vast, created using whatever materials were available nearby. The problem with this type of art is that it can only appear in one place at one time and usually cannot be moved, either because it's in a particular location or because it's so fragile, large or transitory. Natural materials deteriorate rapidly and the changes are often part of the work. Some artists like the transience because it means the work cannot be owned or sold. Many Land artists have felt that the art market stifles artistic expression and affects what artists produce.

Environmental issues

Most Land artists explore the relationships between people and the world around them. Their art may range from piles of boulders to small arrangements of leaves or grass, or it may be recordings of activities or temporary alterations made to the landscape. Richard Long goes for walks in wild and remote parts of the world, recording his travels with maps, poems and photos. Sometimes he leaves his mark by making small changes to the landscape, such as simple arrangements of stones or driftwood, or making imprints on grass, then photographing the result. He often collects objects he finds on his walks and later incorporates them in his sculptures. Andy Goldsworthy works with individual landscapes, from leafy woods to icy plains. After gathering natural materials found close by, such as leaves, pebbles, feathers and ice, he creates arrangements compatible with the surroundings. Robert Smithson built a vast spiral jetty from earth and stones in the Great Salt Lake in Utah. The work was to appear as part of the landscape, yet would also change due to environmental effects.

LAND ART

'Artists are map-makers of human consciousness and of the spiritual world as well as measurers and describers of the natural world.'
Richard Long

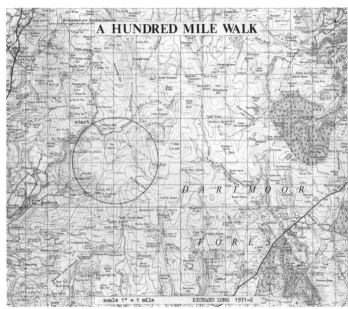

A HUNDRED MILE WALK

scale 1" = 1 mile   RICHARD LONG 1971-2

Day 1   Winter skyline, a north wind

Day 2   The Earth turns effortlessly under my feet

Day 3   Suck icicles from the grass stems

Day 4   As though I had never been born

Day 5   In and out the sound of rivers over familiar stepping stones

Day 6   Corrina, Corrina

Day 7   Flop down on my back with tiredness
        Stare up at the sky and watch it recede

Opposite Andy Goldsworthy, *Storm King Wall* 1997–8, field stone, approx. 1.5 x 694.3 m , Storm King Art Centre, New York
Created over a two-year period, this extensive sculpture was made using stones found close by. Near a small wood Goldsworthy found the remains of a drystone wall and working with a crew of craftsmen, he rebuilt the wall, without mortar or cement, weaving it in and out of the trees. At one point it even emerges on two sides of a pond and snakes across a field.

Top Robert Smithson, *Spiral Jetty* 1970, mud, precipitated salt crystals, rocks, water coil, 4.5 x 457.2 m, Rozel Point, Utah, Collection Dia Art Foundation
In April 1970 Smithson gave instructions for 6,650 tons of earth and rock to be arranged in an anti-clockwise spiral, projecting a quarter of a mile into the Great Salt Lake. His original influences were Minimalists such as Carl Andre, but he moved away from prefabricated industrial materials to using natural processes in natural surroundings.

Bottom Richard Long, *A Hundred Mile Walk* 1971–2, pencil, map, printed text on paper, photographs and labels on board, 21.6 x 48.3, Tate
All Richard Long's work is generated from solitary walks. This piece was created after several days walking in a circle, following grid references he had previously mapped out. The work includes a map showing his location, a photo of part of the landscape, and phrases recording his thoughts and reactions to the landscape on each day of his journey.

Many of the art movements around the 1960s, 1970s and 1980s overlapped with each other. Performance art emerged from Conceptualism and Land art, for instance.

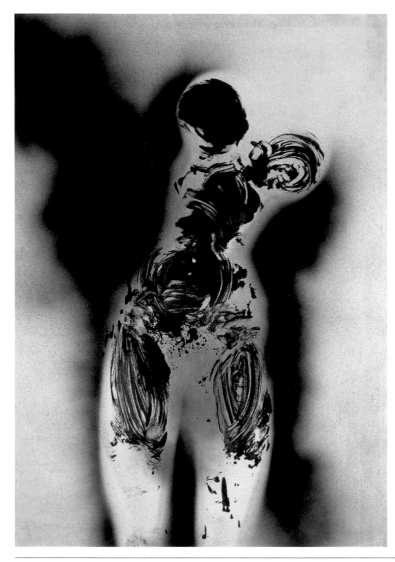

Going with the flow

During the 1960s and 1970s, the distinction between art and theatre blurred. Art performances, which were known as 'happenings' in America and Actionism in Holland, occurred all over the world. The *Anthropometries* of Yves Klein (see p.78) were performances, showing how the boundaries between art, theatre and real life were being obscured. Fluxus was an art movement that began in Germany during the early 1960s. Taken from a Latin word meaning 'to flow,' it revived the crazy spirit of Dada, with artists performing nonsense. Like Dada, Fluxus artists were against commercialism, pretentiousness and materialism of the art world. Although Germany was its principal location, Fluxus was an international avant-garde movement in major Dutch, English, French, Swedish and American cities. Artists enjoyed spontaneity and humour, avoiding any highbrow art theories. Fluxus produced many manifestos, claiming that it wanted to release people from their inhibitions and to 'promote living art, anti-art.' These goals were shared by other Performance artists who all wanted to shake up the art world, which, even after two world wars and umpteen avant-garde movements, retained its old-fashioned attitudes.

Living art

Performance art originated in Futurism and Dada, but later became a part of Conceptual art. Many Performance artists were motivated by the photographs of Jackson Pollock making his Action paintings. Following this, in the late 1950s, Allan Kaprow (1927–2006) organised happenings in New York. These were performances or events that were acted out as art. They had no narrative and usually involved the audience in some way. Key elements were planned, but parts were also improvised. By the mid-1960s other artists such as Bruce Nauman (born 1941) and Joseph Beuys made several performances, often pointing out social and political issues or our relationship with nature. By 1969, Gilbert & George were not only producing large-scale art, but also becoming living sculptures themselves. From the start, Performance and Living art was recorded in photography, film and video, which, like Land art, eventually became the only way it could reach a large audience.

PERFORMANCE ART & ARTE POVERA

'Performance art can involve the audience with taste, smell and sounds not available with electronic media and not practical with conventional theatre.'
Jack Bowman

Arte Povera

In 1967 the Italian art critic and curator, Germano Celant, described the work of several young Italian artists based in Genoa, Milan, Rome and Turin as 'Arte Povera.' All the artists he described were working in new ways, breaking with the past completely. The years following the Second World War were fraught with economic and political instability in Italy and Arte Povera, with its unrestricted experimentation, ignored the traditions of Italian art. Arte Povera does not mean poor art, but art that is still being created and explored. The artists all worked in many different ways. They painted, sculpted, took photographs and made performances and installations, using both new and old materials, manmade and natural. They explored the processes of making art and considered the relationship between art and life. The attitude of viewers was just as important to them as the processes of making themselves. Artists included Giovanni Anselmo (born 1934), Luciano Fabro (1936–2007), Mario Merz (1925–2003), Marisa Merz (born 1925), Giulio Paolini (born 1940), Michelangelo Pistoletto (born 1933) and Emilio Prini (born 1943).

POLITICAL AGENDA

Performance artists wanted to take their art directly to a public forum, eliminating the need for galleries, agents and any other aspect of capitalism. Many Performance artists had political agendas and wanted to change people's opinions about something – and not just to do with art. For instance, Gilbert & George wanted to change people's preconceptions about homosexuality and Beuys was fiercely opposed to nuclear weapons.

Opposite Yves Klein, *Untitled Anthropometry* 1960, pure pigment and synthetic resin, gold, on paper marouflaged to canvas, 102 x 73, Private collection
Drawn to the blue of the sea and sky around the Mediterranean coast, Klein was fascinated by spiritualism. In his body paintings (*Anthropometries*) he wanted to record physical energy. He used bodies as 'living paint brushes'.

Top Giuseppe Penone, *Breath 5* 1978, fired clay, 154 x 83 x 84, Tate
If you think this is all hot air, you could be right. Penone (born 1947) modelled a piece of clay on the imagined shape of a breath exhaled from his mouth. It includes the shape of the inside of his mouth and, along the side is an impression of his leg, leaning forward, wearing jeans. Penone often considers how humans affect nature and has said that this work is linked with some mythological ideas about the creation of man.

Bottom Mario Merz, *Igloo, Do We Go Around Houses, or Do Houses Go Around Us?* 1977/85, metal, stone, glass, putty and electric light, 266.7 x 500.3 x 1026.1, Tate
Merz was always fascinated by ways that ordinary objects change according to the light or ways in which we perceive them. He was fascinated by architecture and how objects change our sense of space. In 1968 he began working with igloos, as he saw them as ideal organic forms, linked to both ancient cultures and the present. This considers the theme of shelter and the relation of humans to their environment and community.

The term Neo-Expressionism came into use in about 1980 to describe the revival of painting in an Expressionist style. As usual, it developed as a reaction against other art movements, in this case Conceptualism and Minimalism. After so many years of artists concentrating on the big idea and not necessarily the process, the Neo-Expressionists returned to painting recognisable objects (well, vaguely). The movement was also a reaction against new and forceful methods of marketing between art dealers and galleries, which these artists felt discouraged creativity.

FACTS IN A FRAME

INTERNATIONAL IDEAS

In the USA, leading Neo-Expressionists were Philip Guston and Julian Schnabel (born 1951); in Britain the main artists included Christopher Le Brun (born 1951) and Paula Rego (born 1935); in Italy they included Sandro Chia (born 1946) and Francesco Clemente (born 1952); and in Germany they included Anselm Kiefer (born 1945) and Georg Baselitz (born 1938). In Germany the Neo-Expressionists became known as Neue Wilden, which meant 'new Fauves'. In Italy the movement was called Transavanguardia, meaning 'beyond the avant-garde', and in France, a group called Figuration Libre was formed in 1981.

Spontaneous emotion

Using vivid colours inspired by earlier German Expressionists, such as Nolde, Beckmann, Grosz and Munch, the Neo-Expressionists painted their emotions quickly, with strong colour contrasts and distorted subject matter. The paintings were usually large and occasionally incorporated found objects. Artists were more concerned with portraying spontaneous emotions than traditional conventions of precise representation – a lot like the previous Expressionists. And like their predecessors, the artists were focusing on revealing intense feelings and not on realistic technique. Neo-Expressionist paintings, though varied in appearance and content, shared certain qualities. They all rejected traditional standards of composition and design, all created an atmosphere that they thought showed contemporary urban life and modern values, all used vivid and often harsh colour combinations and all had a rough, almost violent, approach. Many of their subjects are gloomy and convey a sense of anxiety and uncertainty. (Depressed? Moi?)

Controversial

Neo-Expressionists claimed that they were opposing the detached and self-conscious abstract art of the 1970s. The movement was also driven by new and aggressive methods of salesmanship, media promotion and marketing by dealers and galleries. Neo-Expressionism was just as controversial as the original Expressionism had been – the public criticised the quality of the work and the fact that it didn't look realistic. There was added disapproval because paintings were produced so quickly and the artists couldn't justify such strong feelings, with no world wars to complain about. If you think about it, the criticisms are quite empty really. Who's to say that painting slowly makes better work, and why should wars be the only way of inspiring strong feelings?

NEO-EXPRESSIONISM

'Art is not a handicraft, it is the transmission of feeling the artist has experienced.'
Leo Tolstoy

Georg Baselitz, *Pillow* **1987, oil on canvas, 200 x 162.2, National Galleries of Scotland**
In 1965, while studying in Florence, Baselitz became fascinated by 16th-century Italian Mannerism; he then gradually developed his figurative painting using bright colours and expressive brushstrokes. He felt strongly about the political problems in Germany, and this is probably why the head here is detached from the rest of its body. Also, the style, brushstrokes and garish colours suggest violence.

Christopher Le Brun, *Dream, Think, Speak* **1981–2, oil on canvas, 244 x 228.5, Tate**
Taking inspiration from 19th-century Romanticists and Symbolists as well as from Expressionists and European myths and folk tales, Le Brun's work appears mysterious and quite vague. He wanted his work to be open to interpretation and not tied to his own explanation. Several of his works include fabled winged horses. This painting, although vague, suggests religious, mythical and literary connections.

Feeling dizzy? First artists reacted against representational art, then they reacted against abstract art and then back again. They either represented the human figure or pointedly ignored it. Unusual materials were used, or usual materials were used unusually. And then, in the middle of all that change, there were artists who went right back to using paint to represent figures. Now fancy that.

So what happened? Well, here are three artists who have painted figures for the last sixty years. Art was never going to return to the realistic endeavours of artists before photography, though. That's certainly not what they were trying to do.

Nightmarish imagery

Artists who painted the human figure in the mid- to late 20th century were usually trying to convey messages. In the 1950s Francis Bacon shocked the international art world with his bold, severe and nightmarish figures. He began painting, then in the 1930s he worked as a furniture and interior designer, but he carried on painting with his friends Lucian Freud (born 1922) and Graham Sutherland (1903–80). Within 15 years his figures were abstracted, disturbing and created to make viewers reconsider their own emotions and figurative paintings in general. He wanted his figures to affect viewers 'violently and poignantly'. Freud, on the other hand, began painting figures – mainly his friends and family – quite realistically, but unflatteringly, and explored the textures and colours of flesh to try to expose our inner fears and feelings. As he developed, he began applying thicker, impasto oil paint, actually creating texture on the canvas. This was to make viewers think about texture, contour and radiance of skin, but also to show each sitter as a living, breathing, imperfect person.

Human mysteries

Paula Rego's work has a sense of enchantment mixed with realism. She uses rich imagery and symbolism to create mysteries for viewers to work out. Much of her work is autobiographical, drawn from her own childhood memories and often including hints of ancient myths or disturbing mixtures of religion, control, happiness, discontentment and passion. Her style is quite graphic and bold and her figures are strongly modelled, usually with one strong light source. All three of these artists show us human dramas; we can look at the canvases and identify with figures depicted on them.

BACON, FREUD & REGO

'The job of the artist is always to deepen the mystery.'
Francis Bacon

Paula Rego, *The Dance* 1988, acrylic on paper on canvas, 212.6 x 274, Tate
During the 1980s Rego created paintings inspired by her early life in Portugal. This painting represents the stages of her life, from childhood to old age. The rhythmic movement of the figures contrasts with the stillness of the setting, and the painting has an eerie, dream-like quality, enhanced by the different proportions of the people. Each dancing group shows Rego – as a child, as a young woman in love, as a married woman and finally, the largest, loneliest figure – as a widow. Her husband had died whilst she was painting this picture.

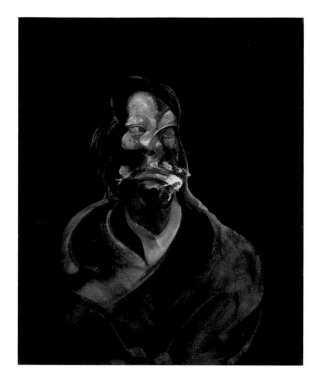

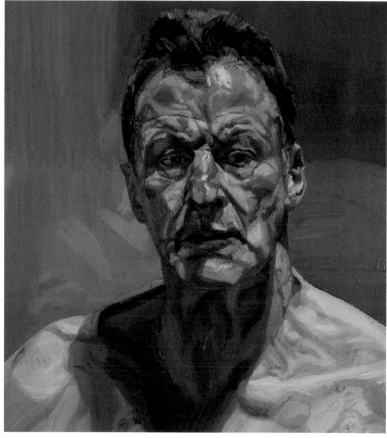

**Francis Bacon, *Portrait of Isabel
Rawsthorne* 1966, oil on canvas,
81.3 x 68.6, Tate**
Although a traditional portrait size and
shape, this smeared and blurred image
seems almost to be dissolving. This is one
of the many paintings Bacon made of his
friend, the artist Isabel Rawsthorne.
Although he knew her well, he worked
from photographs, and with sweeping
brushstrokes distorted her image while
subtly capturing an impression of her.

**Lucian Freud, *Reflection (Self-Portrait)*
1985, oil on canvas, 56 x 51, Private
collection**
Freud was 63 when he painted this
self-portrait. It was at this time that he
began painting the textures and tones
of skin in dramatic and colourful detail.
The glaring light exaggerates the folds
on his face as he looks at us with a wise,
perceptive stare. The paint is applied
thickly, leaving raised areas and rough
patches on the canvas. Freud was
concerned with showing harshness
of appearances and also the harshness
of life.

Two artists who were linked with British Pop art in the 1960s, although they rejected the label, were David Hockney (see p.80) and R.B. Kitaj (1932–2007). In 1976, at the height of Minimalism and Conceptualism, Kitaj organised a highly controversial exhibition. In the catalogue he called the artists exhibiting, the 'School of London'. Each one produced figurative paintings. They included Michael Andrews (1928–95), Frank Auerbach (born 1931), Bacon, Freud, Hockney, Howard Hodgkin (born 1932), Leon Kossoff (born 1926) and Kitaj himself, and they inspired a revival of figurative painting.

Flat and gleaming

At the end of 1963 Hockney moved from England to California, inspired by the light and surroundings. In 1971, at his first solo show in London, his work was a great success and he has continued to be successful ever since. Like Picasso, he has changed direction several times, worked as a stage and costume designer; and like Warhol, he has worked in graphic design, print and photography. In England Hockney used oil paints, but since living in California he has worked in acrylics, emphasising their flat, gleaming colours, as well as oils, watercolours and collage. Many of his works are similar to the snapshot photographs he uses as references. Influenced by Picasso and Matisse among others, his energy and various approaches have resulted in large bodies of work in different media. Some elements often recur in his work, however different the styles and materials, such as dramatic perspectives, luminous light and radiant colour.

Exaggerated and agitated

American-born Ron Kitaj, a friend of Hockney, studied in New York, Vienna and England. His brightly coloured figurative paintings with their overlapping planes resembling collages, influenced British Pop art. Calling some of his line drawings 'agitational usage', Kitaj has also been called the world's greatest draughtsman. He often painted chaotic landscapes and impossible three-dimensional structures, along with exaggerated human forms. Unlike Hockney, in the 1960s and 1970s he was not received favourably by critics and the public. One of the reasons for this was that his work was not as easy to look at as was expected from someone with a Pop art background. In his later years he brought his Jewish heritage into his work more, along with references to the Holocaust and to literature, frequently mixed together on one canvas.

HOCKNEY & KITAJ

'If we are to change our world view, images have to change. The artist now has a very important job to do.'
David Hockney

Opposite **R.B. Kitaj,** *The Man of the Woods and the Cat of the Mountains* **1973, oil on canvas, 152.4 x 152.4, Tate**
Drawing on his experiences and memories, Kitaj included references to literature and politics as well as satire in his work. This painting was inspired by a reproduction of an early 19th-century engraving which was a political satire. It's about the relationship between two people – a woman with a cat's body and a man with an ape's body. With its dream-like elements the work is haunting and surreal, and viewers are free to interpret the image as they like.

David Hockney, *A Bigger Splash* **1967, acrylic on canvas, 242.5 x 243.9, Tate**
Painted in California in the early summer of 1967, this shows a hot, sunny, cloudless day – too hot for anyone to be out, except to dive into the cool blue swimming pool and break the silence with a splash. The composition of strong horizontals and verticals is only broken by a few diagonals – the legs of the folding chair, the diving board – and the curves of the splash. Except for the splash, the paint surface is flat: Hockney applied some of the paint with a roller. It's quite a mysterious world – can you actually see the person in the pool?

To recap: Modernism began in about 1850 when many artists began to explore different ways to represent reality. Then in the late 1960s and early 1970s a number of critics noticed that aspects of art and culture seemed to change. The artist Brian O'Doherty (born 1935) wrote in a book, *Art in America*, in 1971 that 'the Modernist era is over'. This led to the conclusion that if Modernism was over, Postmodernism must have begun.

Combination of styles

Several forms of art, including visual art, music and literature, have been classed as Postmodern. It would be easy to say that Postmodernism is anything that was produced after the late 1960s. But things are never that simple and nobody has one clear idea of what exactly Postmodernism is. It's generally accepted to have started with Pop art and included much of what followed, such as Conceptualism, Neo-Expressionism, Feminist art and the Young British Artists of the 1990s. However it's defined, Postmodernism always tries to dissolve the distinction between high culture and mass or popular culture, and to merge the boundaries between art and everyday life. Finally, Postmodern artists refuse to recognise the authority of any single style or definition of what art should be. Their work is often meant to be tongue-in-cheek or quirky, but some of it has been absurd and meaningless. So you can see there are no guidelines for what Postmodernism should be, which makes it almost impossible to define. As far as Postmodernists are concerned, anything can be considered to be art.

Stereotypes

So Postmodernism is not a movement, like, say Cubism or Surrealism. Postmodern artists are often part of other movements or work in diverse areas. Cindy Sherman (born 1954), best known for her self-portraits showing her in different roles, uses photography rather than the traditional artists' medium of painting. Her work explores the representation of women, the nature of art itself and ideas about originality. Some of her pictures take images from cinema, alluding to the stereotyped representation of women in films. Others use images from traditional paintings. Jeff Koons (born 1955) is categorised as a Pop artist but also classed as a Postmodernist. He is noted for his use of brash imagery using painting, sculpture and other forms, often in large scale. Chuck Close (born 1940) achieved fame as a photorealist before a blood clot left him severely paralysed. He continues to paint with a brush strapped to his hand, usually producing gigantic portraits in squares created by an assistant. Viewed from a distance, these squares appear as a complete, photorealistic image.

POSTMODERNISM

'I didn't want to make "high" art, I had no interest in using paint, I wanted to find something that anyone could relate to without knowing about contemporary art.'
Cindy Sherman

Opposite Jeff Koons, *Three Ball Total Equilibrium Tank (Two Dr J Silver Series, Spalding NBA Tip-Off)* 1985, mixed media, 153.6 x 123.8 x 33.6, Tate

During the 1980s several countries saw the growth of consumerism, when many people seemed to seek personal happiness by buying lots of possessions. Koons, who had previously worked as a stockbroker, made a series of works presenting consumer items in glass cases. Removed from any realistic purpose, they become art or museum objects to be viewed differently from their intended function. In America, as in many other countries, sport was a way of achieving fame and fortune. So the basketballs here represent the way the world seemed to be going – people wanting to buy material things to achieve happiness and even celebrity status.

Cindy Sherman, *Untitled #126* 1983, photograph on paper, 182.8 x 121.8, Tate

In all of Sherman's work she reinvents her own image, dressing up in a variety of costumes and taking on the role of stereotyped poses and attitudes. These have been called 'costume dramas' by some. This photograph and others like it resulted from an invitation to do a fashion spread for the American magazine *Interview*. Her photographs for this series are often unattractive, contradicting the traditional aims of fashion photography. Sherman has said that she was 'trying to make fun of fashion'.

In 1988 a group of art students in London organised an exhibition called *Freeze*. Their work was diverse, shocking, and nothing like anyone had ever seen before. You probably think, so what? Loads of art students have exhibitions that people have never seen before (and some you might never want to see again) but the *Freeze* exhibition was different. Damien Hirst (born 1965), who did most of the organising, got several prominent art critics and collectors to come, and a lot of the artists' work was either bought or talked about in the press.

SHOCK FOR SHOCK'S SAKE

The YBAs triggered a lot of anxiety and outrage. Many complain that a lot of the work is created just to shock. There are other concerns too:

- Does the work have a deeper meaning? If so, what?
- If there are meanings, are they worth searching for?
- How can you tell a good idea from a bad one?

Now think of it this way:

- Does it matter if there are no extra meanings?
- Just because you could have done it, does that make the work bad or not art?
- If you could have done it, does it mean you can take part more? (You might think, 'I'd have done it like this' or 'fancy doing that!' and so on).
- Is it meant to be taken seriously? A lot of art is meant to make us smile or even laugh.

YBAs (BRIT ART)

'I don't believe in art. I believe in artists.'
Marcel Duchamp

Shock tactics

These new artists became nicknamed YBAs, for 'Young British Artists'. These days their work is more often called Brit art because the artists aren't that young anymore. They had no conventions or rules and complete freedom over the materials and processes they used. The work was completely diverse and a lot of it shocks and provokes viewers. Brit art stems from Conceptualism (see pp.90–1), Surrealism (see pp.66–7) and Fluxus (see p.94).

Controversial

Brit artists include Hirst, Chris Ofili (see pp.18, 107), Cornelia Parker (born 1956), Sarah Lucas (born 1962), Christine Borland (born 1965), Marc Quinn (born 1964), Gary Hume (born 1962), Tracey Emin (born 1963), Rachel Whiteread (born 1963) and Jenny Saville (born 1970). They all work in diverse materials, including things that can be thrown away – in contrast to art of the past when paintings and sculpture were produced to last. Hirst's work includes wall displays, paintings, installations and glass tanks containing animals in formaldehyde; Ofili creates paintings using materials such as, magazines, sequins and elephant dung; Parker crushes or wraps objects; Lucas has made sculpture from everyday items and Emin has made installations (see pp.107–9) usually focused around her own life. Many of their works became notorious after 1997 when a controversial exhibition of their work called *Sensation* toured London, Berlin and New York.

Opposite Jenny Saville, *Propped*
1992, oil on canvas, 213.4 x 182.9,
Private collection
Focusing on an oversized woman,
Jenny Saville confronts the traditional
female nude in art history. Behind her,
quotations from a French feminist
theorist are etched into the paint surface.
Saville's work is characterised by textured
and multi-coloured brushwork and the
over-sized figure.

Top Gary Hume, *Incubus 1991,*
alkyd house paint on Formica,
238.9 x 384.6, Tate
One of a series of paintings which
Hume based on swing doors found in
schools and hospitals, this life-size
representation is painted in household
gloss paint with shapes to denote
windows and panels on actual doors.
His critics rejected his door paintings as
being about nothing, but he said they
echo the environment they come from
and everything reflected in them
becomes part of the art.

Bottom Damien Hirst, *The Physical
Impossibility of Death in the Mind of
Someone Living* 1991, glass, steel, silicon,
formaldehyde solution and shark, 217 x
542 x 180, Private collection
One of Hirst's most notorious works was
a 14-foot long dead shark in a glass tank.
It offended a lot of people, but he said
that it was to make viewers consider
death when they wouldn't normally.
We don't usually come face-to-face
with dead things and all living things
ultimately die.

In 1984 the first Turner Prize was awarded. It has since become an important annual event that always provokes debate. Founded by a group called the Patrons of New Art to encourage wider interest in contemporary art, they named the prize after the British painter J.M.W. Turner (1775–1851), partly because he himself had wanted to establish a prize for young artists and partly because in his day, his work was controversial.

The shortlist

The Turner Prize is awarded to a British artist under the age of 50, or an artist working in Britain, for an outstanding presentation of their work in the last year. For the first three years the prize money was £10,000. From 1991 to 2003 this was raised to £20,000; in 2004 the value was increased to £40,000.

For the first four years a shortlist of selected artists was announced, then in 1988 the shortlist was not announced publicly and instead of an exhibition of work by them, the winner alone was offered a solo show the following year. By 1991 the shortlist was reinstated, and once again three or four artists were announced as possible winners before the final judging took place. In that same year it was also decided to introduce the age limit of 50, so that younger artists just setting out weren't competing with artists at the height of their careers.

As it is organised by Tate, the exhibition for the Turner Prize is usually held at Tate Britain; in 2007, however, in celebration of the city of Liverpool being named the Capital of Culture, it was held at Tate Liverpool.

PROTEST GROUPS

Since 1991, when the award ceremony was first broadcast live on television, various groups have staged protests. These have included a group called Fanny Adams, protesting against male domination of the art world, the K Foundation (formerly the pop band KLF), who awarded £40,000 to Rachel Whiteread as the 'worst shortlisted artist' in 1993, and FAT (Fashion, Architecture and Taste) who objected to the 'cultural elitism' of the art establishment.

Rachel Whiteread, *Untitled (Nine Tables)* 1998, concrete and polystyrene, 68.1 x 375 x 519, Tate
Rachel Whiteread won the Turner Prize in 1993. She makes casts of objects which have usually been used by humans. She casts the 'negative' space around or beneath these objects, which then become the 'positive' forms of the sculptures. In this work she took a familiar item of furniture, but presented only the memory of its presence. In doing this, she evokes the past of the object as well as the lives of those who once used it.

THE TURNER PRIZE

'The notion that the public accepts or rejects anything in modern art is merely romantic fiction. The game is completed and the trophies distributed long before the public knows what has happened.'
Thomas Wolfe

New media

Intended to promote public discussion about new developments in contemporary art, the Turner Prize is widely recognised as one of the most important and prestigious awards for the visual arts in Europe. Since the age limit was introduced, early winners' paintings now seem conservative in contrast with the Conceptualism and 'new media' work, which became more usual from the 1990s. Artists who have become known for this, and almost synonymous with the Turner Prize, include Rachel Whiteread and Damien Hirst (see pp.104–5). Even those who do not win often achieve recognition and success. For instance, Jake and Dinos Chapman (born 1966 and 1962 respectively) and Mona Hatoum (born 1952) have achieved international renown for their work. Mona Hatoum was shortlisted for the Turner Prize in 1995 and the Chapman brothers were shortlisted for the Turner Prize in 2003.

Tracey Emin, *My Bed* 1998, mattress, linens, pillows and objects, 79 x 211 x 234, Saatchi Gallery, London
Have you ever been moaned at for not making your bed? Tracey Emin has. In 1999, when it was short-listed for the Turner Prize, *My Bed* was exhibited at Tate Britain. There was a furore about its unsuitability and when it didn't win, Emin angrily blamed the media. *My Bed* – an unmade, dirty bed with squalid detritus around it, plus scribbles and embroideries on the surrounding walls – denotes the artist's depression.

Chris Ofili, *No Woman No Cry* 1998, acrylic, oil, resin, pencil, paper collage, Letraset, map pins and elephant dung on linen, 243.8 x 182.8 x 5.1, Tate
As a tribute to the murdered London teenager Stephen Lawrence and the subsequent mishandled police investigation, 1998 Turner Prize winner Ofili painted a woman crying. A collaged image of Stephen Lawrence's face appears in each of her tears, with the words 'R.I.P. Stephen Lawrence' beneath the paint. Ofili also wanted the painting to be a general portrayal of sadness and grief. By experimenting with materials such as elephant dung, he created unexpected contrasts and textures.

From around 1970 there was a change in critical thinking about art. The term 'pluralism' came to describe art that was complex and made by artists who used a range of materials and approaches. Mediums like video, photography and performance challenged the authority of painting and sculpture, and Land art and graffiti art escaped the confines of the art gallery. The view of modern art, with mainstream styles and approaches flowing from one 'ism' to another, had given way to broader and more unrelated works.

The new art styles and approaches that came and went over the late 20th century occurred partly because artists wanted to explore new ideas and make something original, and partly because attitudes to art were changing. Movements now emerged faster than before, which is why it's often hard to keep up and why so many movements overlap with each other.

GENERATION ME

In the late 20th century, particularly in affluent nations, a general 'I come first' attitude spread among young people. Roughly described as anyone born after the 1970s, the 'Me Generation' became less public-spirited and focused on putting their own needs before anyone else's. The trouble is that people's expectations for themselves have often been far greater than they could achieve, and the result has been more depression, anxiety and loneliness. Many things have been blamed for this self-centred attitude, including science, the media – and modern art.

PLURALISM

'One doesn't make art for other people, even though I am very concerned with the viewer.'
Anish Kapoor

The installation

As people became bombarded with images from increasingly sophisticated media, many artists found traditional methods of art insufficient for their purposes. The search for more immediate and all-embracing materials led to the idea of the installation. This is a combination of various objects and materials displayed in one space. There are usually several aspects to each installation – not just one painting or statue, but several ideas and objects making up a whole work. In a way this has helped art to become more a part of life – people can really feel part of installations and judge for themselves whether it's good or bad art. Installations are often constructed in museums and galleries or in towns or the public environments. Any materials can be used, such as natural or manmade materials and new media such as video, sound recordings or the internet. There is no longer that clear-cut differentiation between the art and us. Pluralism wasn't a movement you see, and a lot of the art we've been looking at falls into the pluralism category.

Opposite **Ron Mueck,** *Ghost* **1998, fibreglass, silicon, polyurethane foam, acrylic fibre and fabric, 201.9 x 64.8 x 99.1, Tate**
Australian born son-in-law of Paula Rego (see p.98), Ron Mueck (born 1958) began his career as a puppet maker. Currently, he produces figurative sculpture in a hyper-realist style but either enlarged or diminished. His human subjects look eerily real, all based on friends and relatives. The distorted size and awkward posture emphasises this girl's emotional state.

Above left **Rebecca Horn,** *Ballet of the Woodpeckers* **1986, mixed media, Tate**
Originally created for the entrance hall of a theatre inside a Viennese psychiatric clinic, German sculptor and film-maker Rebecca Horn (born 1944) wanted to make patients and visitors feel connected through mirrored images. Small hammers 'peck' against the mirrors in constantly changing rhythms, sounding like woodpeckers. One hammer taps into charcoal and the dust falls into a mound, settling on an egg suspended just above the floor. As in many of her works, she makes viewers become the focus of the action.

Above right **Anish Kapoor,** *Ishi's Light* **2003, fibreglass, resin and lacquer, 315 x 250 x 224, Tate**
Bombay-born British sculptor Anish Kapoor (born 1954) makes mystical sculptures infused with both Western and Eastern cultures using diverse materials and bright colours. This work is named after his son, Ishan. An egg-like structure opens to reveal a dark red interior; through reflections from the curved interior a column of light appears at the centre. As in all his works, Kapoor explores ideas about space, blurring the boundaries between visible and invisible.

The first digital pictures were made in the 1960s by scientists with complex machines. Home computers appeared in the 1980s as suddenly as photography had appeared in the 1830s. And just as photography had been either loved or hated by artists in those days, at first, artists either loved or hated computers – or just didn't think they could be anything to do with art. Digital art can be purely computer-generated, or parts can be taken from another source, such as a scanned image or an image drawn using a special software program. Critics have complained that there is too much emphasis on computer-generated artwork in the world but digital art is beginning to be accepted as the established art community realises that it is not easy to produce. (Oh-ho, that old chestnut – if it's easy, it can't be art, can it?)

Computer crazy

Digital photography and digital printing are now acceptable methods of creation, and internationally many museums are starting to collect digital art. Computer-generated imagery (CGI) is big in the film industry and getting better at creating realistic three-dimensional animated images – which brings us back to artists trying to create lifelike images from the world around us.

Reaching a wider world

The World Wide Web was launched in 1989 by British scientist Timothy Berners-Lee (born 1955). By the mid-1990s it had become a forum for art. Interactivity is a major feature of Internet art and rather than confining art to just galleries and museums, it can now be seen by anyone who has access to the Web. Artists put together images, sound, text and movement, while viewers can interact with the work, dissolving the boundaries between artist and viewer. Heath Bunting (born 1966), who started irational.org in 1994, has explored the interconnections of the Web and the potential of viewer participation. His *BorderXing Guide* website contains documentation of walks that cross boundaries without interruption from customs, immigration or border police. The work comments on the way in which movement between borders is restricted by governments. Dirk Paesmans (born 1965) and Joan Heemskerk (born 1968) work together producing digital art on the internet under the name of Jodi. With backgrounds in photography, video and Performance art, they create Internet art as well as modifying artistic computer games and producing Software art. Since 2002, they have been producing videos in what has been called their 'screen grab' period. A lot of their work, although complex to produce, is light-hearted and has been included in many international exhibitions and festivals.

What next?

Internet artists come from numerous backgrounds and the internet is developing extremely rapidly – these and other factors make it hard to define what makes good Internet art and whether ultimately it will be as durable as other art has been in the past. But if there's one thing we've learned, it's this: it doesn't matter. Enjoy!

DIGITAL ART

'Technology has become the body's new membrane of existence.'
Nam June Paik

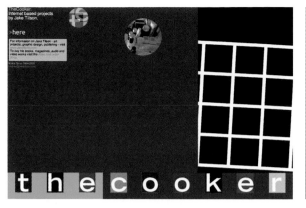

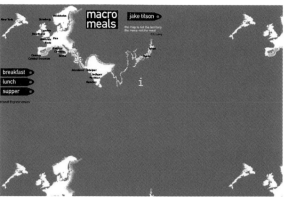

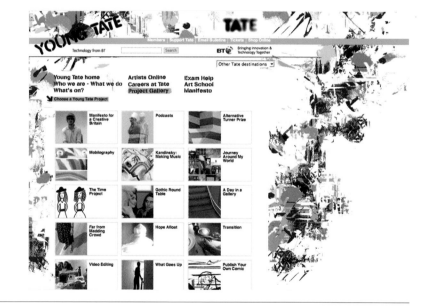

c.1822	Machine-produced pens replace the quill
1825	First passenger railway
1830s	Photography invented
1841	John Rand patents collapsible tin paint tubes
1848	Communist manifesto written in Russia
1874	First Impressionist group exhibition
1879	First practical electric light bulb
1880s	Art Nouveau / Seurat develops pointillism / Cézanne paints from several viewpoints simultaneously
1886	Karl Benz patents first petrol engine car
1888	George Eastman starts manufacturing Kodak cameras / van Gogh and Gauguin paint in bright colours in southern France
1889	The Eiffel Tower is built in Paris
1897	Vienna Secession is formed / the Tate Gallery is founded as the National Gallery of British Art
1900	Psychoanalyst Sigmund Freud publishes *The Interpretation of Dreams*
1903	First successful powered flight taken by the Wright Brothers in the USA
1905	Fauvism / Brücke founded
1907	Start of Cubism
1909	First Futurist manifesto / plastic invented
1910	Kandinsky begins experimenting with abstraction / Mexican Revolution
1911	Kandinsky and Marc found Der Blaue Reiter in Germany / Metaphysical art (pittura metafisica)
1912	Introduction of collage technique to Cubism / Orphism
1913	Malevich begins working on Suprematism / Duchamp produces the first readymade
1914	Vorticism founded
1914–18	First World War
1916	Dada formed
1917	Russian Revolution / Duchamp's *Fountain* is hidden from view at the Society of Independent Artists' exhibition / De Stijl / Neo-Plasticism
1919	Bauhaus founded in Weimar / Harlem Renaissance
1920	Art Deco / Mexican Muralism
1921	Constructivism formed – their first manifesto published

TIMELINE

1923	New Objectivity (Neue Sachlichkeit)
1924	Surrealism launched with publication of André Breton's manifesto
1928	The world's first colour television transmission
1929	The Museum of Modern Art is opens in New York
1936	Spanish Civil War
1937	Nazi exhibition of 'Degenerate Art'
1939–45	Second World War
1946	Abstract Expressionism
1950s	Acrylic paints invented / Colour Field painting / Hard Edge painting / Kinetic art
1956	Pop art / Op art
1959	The Solomon R. Guggenheim Museum opens in New York
1960s	Land art / Minimalism / Conceptualism / happenings / Performance art
1961	New Realism / Fluxus
1965	Video art
1967	Germano Celant coins the term 'Arte Povera'
1969	First man on the moon
1970s	Postmodernism
1975	Microsoft personal computers available
1976	School of London
1979	Macintosh personal computers available
1980	Neo-Expressionism (Transavanguardia/Neue Wilden)
1980s	Mass popular use of the internet / wide use of video cameras / graffiti art
1984	First Turner Prize
1985	Saatchi Gallery opens in London
1986	Musée d'Orsay opens in Paris
1992	Brit art
1995	Whitney Museum of American Art acquires its first piece of Internet art
1996	A Video artist wins Turner Prize for the first time
1997	*Sensation* exhibition opens in London, later travelling to Berlin and New York
1999	Stuckism founded – an 'anti-anti-art' movement
2000	Tate Modern opens in London / First Marcel Duchamp Prize awarded to an artist living in France, considered to be 'the' pioneer of contemporary art
2007	First Kandinsky Prize awarded to a contemporary Russian artist

Here is further information about some of the artists mentioned in this book. To find out more about them or about other artists, look at www.tate.org.uk

Carl Andre (born 1935)
American sculptor associated with Minimalism who uses readymade materials, such as bricks, placing them in geometric, repeated shapes.

Giovanni Anselmo (born 1934)
Italian Arte Povera artist who investigates scientific issues, such as gravity, tension, magnetism and energy as well as organic and inorganic materials.

Richard Anuszkiewicz (born 1930)
American Op artist concerned with the optical effects that occur when bright colours are applied to the same geometric arrangements.

Frank Auerbach (born 1931)
German-born, England-based artist, who was initially criticised for his thick application of paint, then later became appreciated for his painterly images and drawing skills.

Hans Arp (1886–1966)
German-French artist who joined the Dada group. He worked as a sculptor, painter and poet and in other media such as torn and pasted paper.

Francis Bacon (1909–1992)
Irish artist with no formal art training who developed a distorted style and became one of Britain's most important 20th-century painters.

Giacomo Ballà (1871–1958)
Italian painter associated with Futurism, creating images of light, movement and speed. In 1910 he also designed Futurist furniture and clothing.

Georg Baselitz (born 1938)
German-born figurative painter associated with Neo-Expressionism, who spent fifteen years painting everything upside down to make viewers focus on the purely abstract aspects of paintings.

Max Beckmann (1884–1950)
German painter, printmaker, sculptor and writer who rejected being called an Expressionist. In the 1920s he was associated with New Objectivity (Neue Sachlichkeit).

Joseph Beuys (1921–1986)
German artist who turned to art after the Second World War and became well-known in the 1960s, especially for his public performances and for wrapping things in felt.

Peter Blake (born 1932)
British painter and pioneer of Pop art. One of his best-known pieces is the cover of The Beatles' album, *Sergeant Pepper's Lonely Hearts Club Band.*

Umberto Boccioni (1882–1916)
Italian painter and sculptor who helped to write the Futurists' Technical Manifesto with Marinetti; he was killed falling from a horse during the First World War.

David Bomberg (1890–1957)
English painter who produced a series of complex geometric compositions combining the influences of Cubism and Futurism, using a limited palette. After the First World War he developed a more Expressionist technique.

Louise Bourgeois (born 1911)
French sculptor who used her mathematics training to help her early Cubist drawings. She worked as an assistant to Fernand Léger and in her seventies became a successful artist, producing large-scale sculptures.

Constantin Brancusi (1876–1957)
Romanian sculptor based in Paris who was invited by Rodin to be his assistant, but declined, saying: 'No other trees can grow in the shadow of an oak.' He created smooth, simple forms which he believed were at the heart of nature.

Georges Braque (1882–1963)
French artist who worked as a house painter, studied art and worked closely with Picasso: together they pioneered Cubism. In 1912, Braque became the first artist to include collage in a painting.

Marcel Breuer (1902–1981)
Hungarian architect and designer who became director of the furniture department at the Bauhaus and pioneered mass-produced furniture using bent steel tubes as frames.

Heath Bunting (born 1966)
British artist, who is a pioneer of net art, using the internet to explore boundaries and restrictions. See www.irational.org

Victor Burgin (born 1941)
English artist and writer who became associated with Conceptualism in the late 1960s. He has worked with photography and film, and his work is influenced by philosophy.

Anthony Caro (born 1924)
British sculptor best known for his huge abstract works made from girders and sheet metal, welded together and painted in one colour. Recently he has returned to using more traditional materials.

Carlo Carrà (1881–1966)
Italian painter and leading figure of the Futurist movement. In addition to his many paintings, he wrote a number of books about art.

Paul Cézanne (1839–1906)
French painter who abandoned his law studies to become an artist. Originally associating with the Impressionists in Paris, he later returned to his home in southern France where his experiments with perspective influenced the development of Cubism.

Marc Chagall (1887–1985)
Russian-born painter whose work shows influences of Cubism and Expressionism as well as his Jewish heritage. His unusual way of expressing his feelings and imagination on canvas attracted the avant-garde.

Chapman brothers, Jake (born 1966) **and Dinos** (born 1962)
English conceptual artists who came to prominence as Young British Artists during the 1990s and always work in collaboration with each other.

Sandro Chia (born 1946)
Italian painter, printmaker and sculptor who referred to his early work as 'mythical conceptual art' and soon established himself as a major part of the Italian figurative Transavanguardia movement.

Christo and Jeanne-Claude (both born 13th June 1935)
American artists who produce large-scale outdoor works, using mostly fabric. They pay all their own expenses, accepting no sponsorship, commissions or public funds. See www.christojeanneclaude.net

Chuck Close (born 1940)
American painter, associated with Photorealism and known for his massive, detailed and lifelike portraits. After becoming disabled in 1988 he adopted a looser, more colourful style.

ARTISTS

Michael Craig-Martin (born 1941)
Irish sculptor and painter who was influenced by Minimalism. He taught many of the YBAs at Goldsmiths College in London.

Salvador Dali (1904–1989)
Spanish painter who became a Surrealist and once called his paintings, 'hand-painted dream photographs'. Flamboyant and eccentric, he also made films and sculpture and worked with fashion designer Elsa Schiaparelli.

Giorgio de Chirico (1888–1978)
Greek-Italian painter who founded *pittura metafisica* art movement, meaning metaphysical or dream-like art. He painted deserted cityscapes with exaggerated perspective and shadows.

Robert Delaunay (1885–1941)
French painter who originally trained as a decorator. His works reflected his interest in colour theories and Cubism and were among the first abstract images, forming a basis for Orphism.

Sonia Delaunay (née Terk) (1885–1979)
Ukrainian-French artist who co-founded Orphism, with its strong colours and geometric shapes, with her husband Robert. Her work extended to painting, textile and stage set design.

André Derain (1880–1954)
French painter and leader of several avant-garde art movements. He studied with Matisse and became known as a Fauve, but later experimented with Cubism and also designed set decorations and woodcuts.

Jessica Dismorr (1885–1939)
English painter and illustrator who developed a Fauvist style, but after meeting Wyndham Lewis joined the Vorticist movement. Later her work became completely abstract.

Otto Dix (1891–1969)
German Expressionist influenced by van Gogh and the Futurists. He became famous for his unique and grotesque style, usually satirical and commenting on social corruption. Hitler's Nazi regime destroyed many of his works.

Theo van Doesburg (1883–1931)
Dutch painter, poet and architect whose early work was influenced by Post-Impressionism, but after he met Mondrian in 1915, he turned to geometric abstraction. He is best known as the founder and leader of De Stijl.

Aaron Douglas (1899–1979)
American painter and a major figure in the Harlem Renaissance, his style is flat with hard edges and repetitive designs and heavily influenced by African sculptures, jazz music, dance and geometric forms.

Arthur Wesley Dow (1857–1922)
American painter, printmaker, photographer and influential arts educator whose ideas were quite revolutionary for the period. He taught many of America's leading artists, including Georgia O'Keeffe.

Marcel Duchamp (1887–1968)
French artist whose early paintings were influenced by Cubism. He became a leader of Dadaism and Surrealism. His 'readymades' had a profound effect on people's views of art and on future art movements and attitudes.

Raymond Duchamp-Villon (1876–1918)
French sculptor and brother of artists Jacques Villon and Marcel Duchamp, who was instrumental in promoting the Cubists.

Raoul Dufy (1877–1953)
French painter in oil and watercolour, illustrator and designer who was influenced at first by Impressionism, then from 1905 by Fauvism and Cubism.

Tracey Emin (born 1963)
English artist of Turkish Cypriot origin. One of the YBAs whose art takes many different forms including needlework and sculpture, drawing, video, photography and painting.

Jacob Epstein (1880–1959)
American-born sculptor who worked chiefly in the UK, where he pioneered modern sculpture, often producing controversial works that challenged taboos concerning what public artworks appropriately depict.

Max Ernst (1891–1976)
German painter, sculptor, graphic artist and poet, one of the main Dadaists and Surrealists who also made collages and frottages. A friend of Arp and Macke, he was influenced by Cézanne, Munch, Picasso and van Gogh.

Luciano Fabro (1936–2007)
Italian Arte Povera artist who used a diversity of media to explore contrasts between man-made and natural objects and organic and inorganic materials.

Lyonel Charles Feininger (1871–1956)
German-American painter associated with the Expressionist groups Brücke and Der Blaue Reiter. He designed the cover for the 1919 Bauhaus manifesto and taught at the Bauhaus for several years.

Dan Flavin (1933–1996)
American Minimalist famous for creating sculptural objects and installations from commercially available fluorescent light fittings.

Lucian Freud (born 1922)
German-born British painter, grandson of psychologist Sigmund Freud, who specialises in large-scale portraits and figures of people in his life. In close-up, his later technique explores the colours, tones and textures of flesh.

Naum Gabo (1890–1977)
Russian-born American sculptor and painter associated with the Suprematists. He and his elder brother **Antoine Pevsner** (1886–1962) wrote the Constructivist Manifesto. His sculptures explore the idea of space.

Anya Gallaccio (born 1963)
British artist, classed as one of the YBAs in the 1990s, who uses organic materials, such as fruit, vegetables and flowers, which wither, rot and melt as part of her installations. She says her work is both performance and collaboration because of the unpredictable nature of the materials she works with. In 2003, she was shortlisted for the Turner Prize.

Henri Gaudier-Brzeska (1891–1915)
French sculptor with a rough style of direct carving. He moved to England and became involved with Vorticism. Fascinated by primitive sculpture, he advocated that sculpture should show tool marks as a fingerprint of the artist. He was killed in the First World War at the age of 23.

Paul Gauguin (1848–1903)
French painter who longed for a simple life; he left Paris to live in Tahiti and developed paintings with powerful colour and composition.

Mark Gertler (1891–1939)
British painter whose parents were Polish-Jewish immigrants. He studied in London with Stanley Spencer and much of his work was inspired by classical sculpture. Depressed by ill health and the unpopularity of his work, he committed suicide at the age of 48.

Alberto Giacometti (1901–1966)
Swiss sculptor and painter whose earliest works were inspired by Cubism, then in the late 1920s he became involved with the Surrealists. From the late 1940s onwards he created the elongated, emaciated figures for which he is best known.

Gilbert & George
Italian-born Gilbert Proesch (born 1943) and English George Passmore (born 1942), have worked almost exclusively as a pair and were initially known as Performance artists, always wearing identical suits. Later works have included films and large photomontages, often including shocking material.

Vincent van Gogh (1853–1890)
Dutch-born, he spent most of his life in France. Influenced by Impressionism, he began applying swirling brush marks in intense colours. Despite his severe health problems, his painting was original and he was one of the first artists to move art away from the need to make images look real.

Andy Goldsworthy (born 1956)
Scottish artist who makes sculptures from natural materials, usually in the open air and often designed to be temporary.

Arshile Gorky (1904–1948)
Armenian-born American painter who was influenced by Braque, Cézanne and Picasso and had a significant influence on Abstract Expressionism. In the 1940s he was influenced by the Surrealists, particularly Miró. After a succession of personal tragedies, Gorky committed suicide at the age of 44.

Juan Gris (1887–1927)
Spanish painter and sculptor who lived and worked in France most of his life, he was one of the pioneers of Cubism. In the 1920s Gris designed costumes and scenery for Diaghilev's Ballets Russes. He also completed some of the boldest landscapes and still lifes in his Cubist style.

George Grosz (1893–1959)
German draughtsman and painter whose satirical works emerged from his traumatic experiences in the First World War. Between 1918 and 1920 he became a leading member of the Berlin Dada group.

Philip Guston (1913–1980)
American painter who began as a mural artist and turned to Abstract Expressionism, then returned to figurative painting, using a strong, cartoon-like style to comment on the social issues of the day.

Richard Hamilton (born 1922)
English painter, printmaker and writer and one of the pioneers of Pop art, best known for his montages of advertising and contemporary life, especially with his 1956 collage, *Just What Is It that Makes Today's Homes So Different, So Appealing?*

Mona Hatoum (born 1952)
Lebanese Performance artist who moved to London in 1975, produced performance work in the 1980s then moved to mechanical installations, involving video, light and sound. She has often made powerful references to the weaknesses of our bodies.

Joan Heemskerk (born 1968)
Dutch internet artist who works with Dirk Paesmans as 'Jodi' to produce complex and humorous works, intended to confuse and amuse viewers.

Barbara Hepworth (1903–1975)
British sculptor who began working in wood, stone and bronze, originally basing her work on natural forms, but later often creating works that were entirely abstract.

Damien Hirst (born 1965)
British sculptor, painter and designer, prominent YBA with a talent for self-promotion who became famous for preserving dead animals in formaldehyde; he is also well known for his 'spot' paintings.

David Hockney (born 1937)
British painter, draughtsman, printmaker and photographer who achieved success in his early twenties. His art is often autobiographical and although he changes his style frequently, his work is usually colourful and light-hearted.

Howard Hodgkin (born 1932)
English painter, printmaker and collector who paints figurative paintings, which are generally small in scale, refer to his memories, and are quite obscure, inviting viewers to work out what they see.

Edward Hopper (1882–1967)
American painter and printmaker, known for his oil paintings of hotels, motels, trains, roads, restaurants, theatres, cinemas and offices, stressing the theme of loneliness. There is often a cinematic quality to his work.

Rebecca Horn (born 1944)
German installation artist who combines a variety of media: video, performance and sculpture. Since the early 1970s she has been involved in filmmaking, but is particularly famous for her body 'adaptations.'

Gary Hume (born 1962)
British painter, categorised as one of the YBAs in the 1990s, who uses a bright palette and reduced imagery. He focuses on surfaces and minimal and abstract forms.

Alexej von Jawlensky (1864–1941)
Russian Expressionist painter active in Germany who was a member of Der Blaue Reiter and Die Blaue Vier. Colourful at first, when he moved towards abstraction his work became more simplified.

Jasper Johns (born 1930)
American painter, associated with Pop art, who uses recognisable things such as flags, maps and targets, but emphasises their painterly qualities to show that they are art and not everyday objects.

William H. Johnson (1901–1970)
African-American painter associated with the Harlem Renaissance, who lived and worked in New York, France and Denmark. His style and subject matter were wide-ranging. He was influenced by the Expressionists as can be seen by his intense colours and expressive painting technique.

ARTISTS

Donald Judd (1928–1994)
American sculptor and writer who made free-standing works of precise geometrical forms in wood, metal and sometimes coloured Perspex.

Frida Kahlo (1907–1954)
Mexican painter influenced by Realism, Symbolism, Surrealism and the indigenous cultures of Mexico. She used bright colours and painted many self-portraits that express her own pain symbolically.

Wassily Kandinsky (1866–1944)
Russian painter, printmaker and art theorist, recognised as painting the first modern abstract works. He studied Theosophy and believed that art did not need further meaning. He was a founder member of Der Blaue Reiter and taught at the Bauhaus from 1922.

Anish Kapoor (born 1954)
British sculptor of Indian birth who explores spiritual and mythological significances in both Western and Eastern culture. He works with vivid colours and natural materials, focusing on qualities of interior balance and well-being.

Allan Kaprow (1927–2006)
American painter and a pioneer in Performance art who organised the first 'happenings' in New York in the late 1950s and 1960s.

Ellsworth Kelly (born 1923)
American abstract painter, lithographer and sculptor linked to Hard-edge and Colour Field painting and Minimalism. His works emphasise simplicity of form through bright colours.

Anselm Kiefer (born 1945)
German painter and sculptor whose large, textured works include materials like straw, clay and lead. He explores German history and the horror of the Holocaust as well as some of the concepts of Kabbalah.

Ernst Ludwig Kirchner (1880–1938)
German Expressionist painter and printmaker, influenced by the Fauves and by primitive art, he was one of the founders of Brücke. In 1933, his work was branded 'degenerate' by the Nazis, and this was a contributing factor to his suicide.

Ron B. Kitaj (1932–2007)
American painter who spent most of his life in England and was associated with Pop art in the 1960s, using film and photographic images. His later work explores his Jewish heritage.

Paul Klee (1879–1940)
Swiss painter and etcher, best known for his light-hearted attitude to art. He was fascinated by children's painting, believing that there was another world more real than this. He became associated with Der Blaue Reiter and taught at the Bauhaus. In later years he suffered from a condition called scleroderma, and as a result his paintings became dark and bitter.

Yves Klein (1928–1962)
French artist who worked with natural substances such as pure pigment and gold leaf. He patented his own shade of blue, IKB (International Klein Blue) and staged performances.

Gustav Klimt (1862–1918)
Austrian artist who was a leading Viennese Secessionist and had a great influence on decorative art.

Käthe Kollwitz (1867–1945)
German painter, printmaker and sculptor whose work expressed sympathy for the less fortunate, including victims of poverty, hunger and war.

Jeff Koons (born 1955)
American artist renowned for his use of kitsch imagery. He works with painting, sculpture and other forms, often in large scale, focusing on questions of what is 'good taste' in art.

Willem de Kooning (1904–1997)
Dutch Abstract Expressionist, influenced by Cubism, Surrealism and Picasso and best known for a series of paintings of women, made with slashing strokes and dripping paint. The meaning of these images is still disputed.

Joseph Kosuth (born 1945)
American Conceptual artist who explores the nature of art, focusing on ideas and reasons why we produce and look at art.

Christopher Le Brun (born 1951)
English painter, sculptor, draughtsman and printmaker whose expressive work features mythological and dream-like imagery.

Fernand Léger (1881–1955)
French painter, counted as one of the three major Cubists and the first to experiment with abstraction, who painted in a clean, precise and mechanical style after the First World War.

Tamara de Lempicka (1898–1980)
Polish painter born to a wealthy family who moved to Paris where avant-garde artists, particularly Léger and Cézanne, influenced her work. Her work shows influences of Cubism and the prevailing Art Deco style.

Wyndham Lewis (1882–1957)
Canadian-born British painter, author and co-founder of the Vorticist movement. Interested in Japanese prints, Cubism, Futurism and Expressionism, he produced semi-abstract work based on machines and architecture.

Roy Lichtenstein (1923–1997)
American Pop artist who painted in an Abstract Expressionist style from 1957 to 1961, but later painted pictures based on oversized comic strip images using dramatic composition and large dots.

Richard Long (born 1945)
English sculptor, photographer and painter associated with Land art. From the 1970s he produced work as the result of long walks in remote places. Retaining a respect for nature, he uses a variety of methods to demonstrate his experiences in museums or galleries.

Sarah Lucas (born 1962)
British sculptor, installation artist and photographer, who was named one of the YBAs in the 1990s. Her work uses everyday objects to confront sexual stereotyping.

August Macke (1887–1914)
German painter, one of the leading members of Der Blaue Reiter and initially influenced by Impressionism and Post-Impressionism. He later went through a Fauve period, and experimented with Orphism. His greatest work represents feelings and moods, often distorting colour and form.

René Magritte (1898–1967)
Belgian Surrealist painter who, under the influence of de Chirico, began to explore ways of creating a poetic, disturbing effect by depicting recognisable objects in odd settings or in unnatural sizes.

Kasimir Malevich (1878–1935)
Russian painter and designer and a leading pioneer of abstract art who embarked on a completely abstract style in 1915, which he based on pure geometrical elements and called Suprematism.

Franz Marc (1880–1916)
German painter and printmaker who formed Der Blaue Reiter with Macke, Kandinsky and others. Much of his work includes animals in a Cubist style in brightly coloured natural settings.

Henri Matisse (1869–1954)
French artist, known for his fluid style and use of bright colour, who was initially labelled a Fauve. His expressive and colourful work over a half-century won him recognition as one of the leading artists of the 20th century.

Gustav Metzger (born 1926)
Artist and political activist of mixed heritage who developed 'Auto-Destructive Art'; he was also involved with Fluxus.

Amedeo Modigliani (1884–1920)
Italian painter and sculptor, who spent a lot of his life in France, influenced by a range of art movements and styles. He distorted his figures and applied large, flat areas of colour.

Piet Mondrian (1872–1944)
Dutch painter and leading member of De Stijl who evolved a non-representational style which he called Neo-Plasticism, consisting of black grids and the three primary colours.

Henry Moore (1898–1986)
British sculptor influenced by ancient sculpture who carved wood and stone but later produced mainly large bronze castings, often of reclining women or mothers and children in organic, abstracted forms.

Ron Mueck (born 1958)
Australian-born artist who started making models for films and now creates detailed figures, altering their scale to shock and surprise viewers. Mueck is the son-in-law of Paula Rego.

Edvard Munch (1863–1944)
Norwegian painter influenced by van Gogh who created passionate paintings reflecting death and illness of people close to him during his life. His most famous work, *The Scream*, inspired the Expressionists.

Paul Nash (1889–1946)
English landscape painter, wood engraver and official war artist during the First and Second World Wars. With a style influenced by Cézanne and William Blake, his stark landscapes of the Western Front evoked the horrors of war. From 1928 he was increasingly influenced by Surrealism and abstract art.

Barnett Newman (1905–1970)
American Abstract Expressionist painter and sculptor, who began in 1948 to work with fields of colour interrupted by one or more vertical stripes (or 'zips').

Ben Nicholson (1894–1982)
British painter, influenced by Cubism and naïve art. He joined the Abstraction-Création association in Paris in 1933 and explored abstraction, using simplified forms and reliefs.

Emil Nolde (1867–1956)
German painter and printmaker, one of the first Expressionists, a member of Brücke and particularly known for his vigorous brushwork and expressive choice of colours.

Chris Ofili (born 1968)
British artist whose parents came from Nigeria; much of his work draws on African culture. He is known for his decorative work, involving paint and other collage materials, such as glitter and elephant dung.

Georgia O'Keeffe (1887–1986)
American artist whose early works included cityscapes, landscapes and flowers. She later painted landscapes, buildings and bones in New Mexico, helping to pioneer abstract art in the US.

José Clemente Orozco (1883–1949)
Mexican mural painter who was influenced by Symbolism and, often exploring human suffering, was the most complex of the Mexican muralists.

Dirk Paesmans (born 1965)
Belgian internet artist who works with Joan Heemskerk as 'Jodi' to produce complex and humorous works, intended to confuse and amuse viewers.

Cornelia Parker (born 1956)
British artist, who is best known for her large-scale installations and has worked in collaboration with several large institutions. In 1997 she was shortlisted for the Turner Prize.

Francis Picabia (1879–1953)
French painter and writer, one of the major figures of the Dada movement. Rejecting conventional art, he became extremely influential to later artists. His images were complemented by disjointed phrases of no apparent relevance and his work showed influences of Cubism and Dadaism.

Pablo Ruiz Picasso (1881–1973)
Spanish painter, sculptor and child prodigy who developed many different styles of art, in particular Cubism with Braque, inspired by the art of Africa and of Cézanne. He experimented all his life, producing paintings, sculpture, ceramics and stage sets.

Jackson Pollock (1912–1956)
American painter and leading figure of Abstract Expressionism. Originally also influenced by the Mexican muralists, Surrealism and Picasso, by the late 1940s he was painting in a completely abstract way, creating 'drip' paintings by pouring and dripping his paint directly onto the canvas. Action painting like this was similar to Surrealist automatism.

Emilio Prini (born 1943)
Italian Arte Povera artist who explores the relationships between reality and experience using light, photography, sound and text. In his many photographic works, the camera and the processes of photography are the subject of the work.

Marc Quinn (born 1964)
British sculptor associated with Brit art. Many of his works use casts of his own body; he is best known for *Self*, a model of his head made from eight pints of his own blood.

Robert Rauschenberg (1925–2008)
American artist who was influenced by Dada and Surrealism, his work combines painting, collage and readymades.

Paula Rego (born 1935)
Portuguese-born painter and illustrator who has lived in Britain since 1976. She claims that illustrated children's books were her greatest influence. Her paintings explore Portuguese folk art and social conventions.

Ad Reinhardt (1913–1967)
American Abstract Expressionist painter who was most famous for his 'black' or 'ultimate' paintings. He believed in a philosophy he called Art-as-Art and used his writing and satirical cartoons to back the ideas of contemporary abstract artists.

ARTISTS

Gerrit Thomas Rietveld (1888–1964)
Dutch furniture designer and architect who started his own furniture factory in 1911 and designed the famous *Red and Blue Chair* in 1917. He became a member of De Stijl in 1919.

Bridget Riley (born 1931)
One of the leaders of British Op art, who since the mid-1960s has been producing her distinctive, optically vibrant paintings which engage viewers' perceptions, producing subtle visual experiences.

Diego Rivera (1886–1957)
Mexican artist, Communist and husband of Frida Kahlo, whose large wall frescoes helped establish the Mexican Mural Renaissance.

Alexander Rodchenko (1891–1956)
Russian artist who was one of the founders of Constructivism and Russian design. He also worked as a painter and graphic designer before turning to photomontage and photography.

Auguste Rodin (1840–1917)
French artist who modelled the human body with realism and departed from traditional myths and allegories. Although criticised at first, he then had a successful reputation and by 1900 was a world-renowned artist.

Mark Rothko (1903–1970)
Russian-born American painter who was a leading Abstract Expressionist, inspired by Miró and the Surrealists, and later developed Colour Field painting, saturating huge canvases with blocks of colour.

Georges Rouault (1871–1958)
French Fauvist and Expressionist painter and printmaker who painted in a spontaneous style showing contrasting emotions and grotesque figures.

Henri Rousseau (1844–1910)
French naïve painter, best known for his jungle themes. His pictures have a dreamlike, childish style.

Jenny Saville (born 1970)
English painter and YBA who focuses on traditional figurative oil paintings, usually larger than life-size paintings of women, often self-portraits, exploring society's attitudes to women.

Egon Schiele (1890–1918)
Austrian painter, student of Gustav Klimt and a major figurative painter of the early 20th century who produced intense paintings and drawings of people and became associated with Expressionism.

Kurt Schwitters (1887–1948)
German artist associated with Dada who developed a style known as 'Merz', consisting of two- and three-dimensional collages made of rubbish.

Richard Serra (born 1939)
American sculptor of huge abstract works using metal.

Georges Seurat (1859–91)
French painter whose ideas on colour led him to develop pointillism, a technique using tiny dots of pure colour.

Cindy Sherman (born 1954)
American photographic artist who produces pictures that comment on our social attitudes.

Paul Signac (1863–1935)
French Neo-Impressionist who helped to develop pointillism with Seurat. He experimented with various media but luminous colour was the most important aspect of his work. Among others, he inspired Matisse and Derain.

David Alfaro Siqueiros (1896–1974)
Mexican muralist who, with Rivera, Orozco and others, established the 'Mexican Mural Renaissance'.

Karl Schmidt-Rottluff (1884–1976)
German Expressionist and a member of Brücke who focused on natural forms in bold, flattened shapes

Robert Smithson (1938–1973)
American artist who created huge Land art works. He died in an aeroplane crash in Texas while working on one of his artworks.

Stanley Spencer (1891–1959)
British painter known for his expressive and distorted landscapes, portraits and biblical scenes.

Frank Stella (born 1936)
American artist associated with Minimalism. He creates paintings and prints using strips of colour or neutral shades.

Vladimir Tatlin (1885–1953)
Russian painter and architect often called 'the father of Constructivism', who believed that art should be made of industrial materials, such as glass, steel and timber.

Jean Tinguely (1925–91)
Swiss sculptor, best known for his kinetic sculptures – pieces of moving machinery that mocked some ideas of industry.

Wayne Thiebaud (born 1920)
American painter, best known for his colourful still lifes of cakes, pies, sweets and cosmetics. Many later works include landscapes in the same bright, smooth style. Although he has been frequently associated with Pop art due to his choice of subject matter, Thiebaud does not consider himself a Pop artist.

Cy Twombly (born 1928)
American Abstract Expressionist, well known for his large-scale, freely scribbled graffiti paintings on muted backgrounds.

Victor Vasarely (1908–1997)
Hungarian-French artist often called the father of Op art. As a graphic artist in the 1930s he created the first Op art piece, *Zebra*, consisting of curving black and white stripes, indicating the direction his work would take.

Jacques Villon (1875–1963)
French Cubist painter and printmaker, brother of Duchamp and Duchamp-Villon, who invented Orphism.

Maurice de Vlaminck (1876–1958)
French painter, printmaker and author who, with Derain and Matisse, is considered to be one of the principal Fauvists

Andy Warhol (1928–1987)
American artist associated with Pop art. Best known for his repeated prints of images taken from advertising and the media, he also made experimental films.

Rachel Whiteread (born 1963)
British sculptor associated with the YBAs who makes casts of everyday objects, including boxes, fridges and houses.

Abstract Expressionism
Large, abstract paintings produced to show and affect emotions. There are two types: Action painting and Colour Field painting. The movement began in the mid-1940s and lasted until the 1960s and 1970s.

Art Deco
Popular international design movement from 1925 until 1939, affecting the decorative arts including architecture, interior design, fashion and painting. It was a mixture of many different styles and movements of the early 20th century, including Constructivism, Cubism, Modernism, Bauhaus, Art Nouveau and Futurism.

Art Nouveau
International style of architecture, art and design that peaked in popularity from 1890 to 1905 and was characterised by stylised, sinuous designs often incorporating floral and other plant-inspired motifs.

Arte Povera
Italian art movement in which artists use a broad range of materials and a wide range of ideas, but not particularly traditional materials, processes or ideas. The main thrust of the movement was from 1967 to 1972, but it influenced later art hugely.

Bauhaus
Influential German art school where every student studied art, architecture and design with the aim of creating a better living environment for all until the Nazis closed it in 1933.

Colour Field
Originally used to describe the work of the Abstract Expressionists, which was characterised by large canvases saturated with colour; the idea developed in the 1960s when new artists painted in a similar way, but they avoided the concepts of evoking emotional, mythic or religious feelings with it.

Conceptualism
From the late 1960s to the 1970s, Conceptual artists emphasised the ideas inspiring works of art, often as a protest against the commercialism of the art world.

Constructivism
From around 1917 until the early 1920s Constructivists tried to help create a new society after the Russian Revolution by applying geometric design principles to all areas of art and design.

Cubism
Inspired by Cézanne, from about 1907 Picasso and Braque developed a way of depicting the world on two-dimensional surfaces that showed several viewpoints of objects at once so that the objects were described more clearly and honestly.

Dada
During the First World War in neutral Switzerland an anti-art, anti-war movement emerged, involving visual arts, literature, theatre and graphic design. Activities included public gatherings and demonstrations. The movement influenced later styles and movements including Surrealism, Pop art and Fluxus.

De Stijl
Founded in Holland by van Doesburg and Mondrian to promote the use of geometric abstract shapes and primary colours, based on achieving harmony.

Digital art
Digital art is created with digital media and technologies. To produce their work, digital artists use all kinds of electronic information and programs, such as computer graphics software, digital photography technology and computer-assisted painting. Now digital tools have become such an integral part of the art-making process, like Postmodernism, some people say we are now in a post-digital era.

Expressionism
In finding ways to express emotions through exaggeration, vigorous brushstrokes and strong colours, German artists had several versions of Expressionism. Der Blaue Reiter and Brücke were two of the main groups, inspired by, among others, van Gogh and Munch.

Fauvism
Strong colours and slashing brushstrokes earned some artists the nickname 'wild beasts' when they exhibited together at the Salon d'Automne in Paris in 1905. Unlike the German Expressionists, their work was meant to be joyful.

Fluxus
Taken from a Latin word meaning 'to flow,' this was an international network of artists, composers and designers who mixed different materials and approaches in the 1960s.

Futurism
Founded by a poet, this Italian movement's members celebrated the energy and movement of the machine age and city life. They published manifestos, but the First World War put paid to their ideas when several members were killed.

Harlem Renaissance
An African American cultural movement of the 1920s and early 1930s that was centred in the Harlem neighbourhood of New York City. It marked the first time that publishers and critics took African-American literature and art seriously and attracted significant attention.

Impressionism
The first major avant-garde movement, describing several artists who no longer painted traditional subjects in photographic realist style, but captured the effects of fleeting moments and light, using brilliant colours and few details.

Installation art
Art that is created in certain locations, such as the environment, exhibition spaces or on the internet; it is usually temporary and generally intended to make viewers reconsider specific things.

Kinetic art
Moving sculpture, either made with machinery or relying on the surrounding air to move it.

Land art
Also called Environmental art, a movement whose artists explore nature and make records of their visits by building natural, impermanent sculpture, taking photographs or creating other responses to the surroundings.

Living art
More than Performance art, Living artists assume their work throughout their working days. Living art is not usually a one-off 'happening' or event, but is usually a means of expression to encourage viewers to consider something from a different perspective.

MOVEMENTS

Mexican muralism
Revival of large-scale, colourful mural painting in Mexico during the 1920s and 1930s, illustrating social and political messages.

Minimalism
By concentrating on the underlying ideas of art rather than on the art itself, this movement can often seem to be about very little. The work often involves repetition and avoids using traditional creative skills.

Modernism
A series of cultural movements in art and architecture, music, literature and design, which emerged around 1884 to 1914. Artists, believing that people should embrace the industrial age, produced works that rebelled against 'outdated' 19th-century traditions.

New Objectivity
Also known as Neue Sachlichkeit, this was developed in Germany in the early 1920s in opposition to Expressionism. It ended in 1933 with the rise to power of the Nazis.

Op art
Short for Optical art, this refers to a geometric abstract art movement that began in the late 1950s. It aims to affect viewers' perception and create the illusion of movement.

Orphism
A colourful and abstracted aspect of Cubism that was concerned with the expression and significance of sensation, and aimed to dispense with recognisable subject matter and to rely on form and colour alone to communicate meaning.

Performance art
Related to theatrical performance but with no plot or sense of drama, this art is used to make a political or social point, or simply to entertain.

Pluralism
This rejects Modernism, by asserting that all styles of art and cultural forms are comparable.

Pointillism
Also known as divisionism, this was a method of applying small dots of pure colour all over a work, rather than mixing and blending the colours together, so that when the painting is viewed from a distance, the dots react optically to each other, creating more vibrant effects than they would have if the colours had been mixed.

Pop art
Either the celebration or the mocking of Western consumerism after the austere years of the Second World War. The art was not meant to last, but to be as throwaway as the society from which it emerged.

Post-Impressionism
A group of artists who did not work in any one style, but simply worked after Impressionism, moving on the ideas of the Impressionists.

Postmodernism
A reaction to Modernism and greatly influenced by the Second World War, Postmodernism is believed to have started with Pop art and always tries to dissolve the distinction between high culture and mass culture and to merge restrictions of art and life.

Suprematism
Malevich started this idea that art should be about creating geometric abstract shapes that are completely independent of the visible world – like nothing we see around us.

Surrealism
Following Dada and the theories of psycho-analyst Sigmund Freud, this movement explored the world of the unconscious and subconscious mind.

Viennese Secessionism
Formed in 1897 in Vienna, Secessionists rejected the conservative attitude of the Viennese establishment.

Vorticism
A London-based movement inspired by Futurism and Cubism, celebrating the excitement of the machine age. Like Futurism, however, the movement did not survive the First World War.

YBAs (Brit art)
Beginning in the 1990s, a group of conceptual and installation artists based in Britain came to public notice with their shocking approach and irreverence. Initially called Young British Artists, their work is now more often called Brit art.

Here is a list of some of the museums and galleries throughout the world where you can see modern and contemporary art. National and local holidays vary, so check the opening times before you visit.

AUSTRALIA

Gallery of Modern Art
Stanley St
South Brisbane
QLD 4101
Telephone: + 61 7 3840 7303
qag.qld.gov.au

Museum of Contemporary Art
140 George Street
The Rocks
Sydney
NSW 2000
Telephone: + 61 2 9245 2400
www.mca.com.au

BRAZIL

Museu de Arte Moderna
Av Infante Dom Henrique 85
Parque do Flamengo
Rio de Janeiro
20021-140
Telephone: + 55 (21) 2240 4944
www.mamrio.com.br

CANADA

National Gallery of Canada
380 Sussex Drive
Ottawa
Ontario
K1N 9N4
Telephone: + 1 613 990 1985
www.gallery.ca

FRANCE

Musée Picasso
Hôtel Salé
5, rue de Thorigny
Paris 75003
Telephone: + 33 (0)1 42 71 25 21
www.musee-picasso.fr

Musée d'Orsay
62, rue de Lille
75343 Paris Cedex 07
Telephone: + 33 (0)1 40 49 48 14
www.musee-orsay.fr

Centre Pompidou
Place Georges Pompidou
75004 Paris
Telephone: + 33 (0)1 44 78 12 33
www.centrepompidou.fr

GERMANY

Bauhaus-Archiv
Klingelhöferstraße 14
D - 10785 Berlin
Telephone: + 49 (0)30 254 0020
www.bauhaus.de

Brücke-Museum
Bussardsteig 9
14195 Berlin-Dahlem
Telephone: + 49 (0)30 81 2029
www.bruecke-museum.de

GREECE

National Museum of Contemporary Art
Vas. Georgiou B'
17-19 and Rigillis Street
Athens
Telephone: + 30 210 9242 1113
www.emst.gr

IRAN

Tehran Museum of Contemporary Art
Kargar Ave
Park-e Laleh Area
Telephone: +98 8896 5411
www.tehranmoca.com

ITALY

Galleria Nazionale d'Arte Moderna-Arte Contemporanea
Viale delle Belle Arti 131
00196 Rome
Telephone: + 39 06 322981
www.gnam.beniculturali.it

Palazzo Grassi
Campo San Samuele, 3231
30124 Venezia
Telephone: + 39 041 523 16 80
www.palazzograssi.it

Peggy Guggenheim Collection
704 Dorsoduro
I-30123 Venice
Telephone: + 39 041 2405 411
www.guggenheim-venice.it

JAPAN

National Museum of Modern Art
3-1 Kitanomaru-kōen
Chūō-ku
Tokyo
Telephone: + 81 5777 8600
www.momat.go.jp

MEXICO

Diego Rivera Mural Museum
Plaza de la Solidaridad
Balderas and Colón
Mexico City
Telephone: + 5255 5510 2329
www.arts-history.mx/museos/mu

Frida Kahlo Museum
Londres 247
Col. del Carmen
Mexico City, c.p. 04000
Telephone: + 5255 5554 5999
www.museofridakahlo.org

Museo Tamayo Arte Contemporaneo
Reforma y Gandhi
Bosque de Chapultepec
Mexico City, c.p. 11580
Telephone: + 5255 5286 6519/29
www.museotamayo.org

THE NETHERLANDS

Stedelijk Museum
Museumplein 10
1071 DJ Amsterdam
Telephone: + 31 (0)20 573 2911
www.stedelijkindestad.nl

Vanabbemuseum
Bilderdijklaan 10
5611 NH Eindhoven
Telephone: +31 (0)40 238 1000
www.vanabbemuseum.nl

Van Gogh Museum
Postbus 75366
1070 AJ Amsterdam
Telephone: + 31 (0)20 570 5200
www.vangoghmuseum.nl

NORWAY

Munch Museum
Tøyengata 53
0578 Oslo
Telephone: + 47 23 49 35 00
www.munch.museum.no

RUSSIA

State Hermitage Museum
34 Dvortsovaya Naberezhnaya
St Petersburg
190000
Tel: + 7 812 110 90 79
www.hermitagemuseum.org

SINGAPORE

Singapore Art Museum
71 Bras Basah Road
Singapore
189555
Telephone: + 65 6332 23222
www.singart.com

SPAIN

Guggenheim Bilbao
Avenida Abandoibarra, 2
48001 Bilbao
Telephone: + 34 944 35 90 80
www.guggenheim-bilbao.es

Museo Picasso
Palacio de Buenavista
San Agustín, 8
29015 Málaga
Telephone: + 34 902 44 33 77
www.museopicassomalaga.org

WHERE TO SEE MODERN ART

Prado Museum
Paseo del Prado
28014 Madrid
Telephone: + 34 913 30 28 00
www.museodelprado.es

**Museo Nacional Centro de
Arte Reina Sofía**
Santa Isabel, 52
28012 Madrid
Telephone: + 34 917 74 10 00
www.museoreinasofia.es

SWEDEN

Moderna Museet
Exercisplan 4
Skeppsholmen
Stockholm
Telephone: + 46 8 5195 5289
www.modernamuseet.se

TURKEY

Istanbul Modern
Meclis-I Mebusan Caddesi
Tophane
Telephone: + 90 334 7300
www.istanbulmodern.org

UNITED KINGDOM

Saatchi Gallery
Duke of York's HQ
King's Road
London, SW3 4SQ
Telephone: +44 (0)20 7823 2363
www.saatchi-gallery.co.uk

**Scottish National Gallery of
Modern Art**
75 Belford Road
Edinburgh, EH4 3DR
Telephone: + 44 (0)131 550 4100
www.nationalgalleries.org

Tate Liverpool
Albert Dock
Liverpool, L3 4BB
Telephone: +44 (0)151 702 7400
www.tate.org.uk

Tate Modern
Bankside
London, SE1 9TG
Telephone: +44 (0)20 7887 8888
www.tate.org.uk

USA

Albright-Knox Art Gallery
1285 Elmwood Avenue
Buffalo
NY 14222-1096
Telephone: + 1 716 882 8700
www.albrightknox.org

The Art Institute of Chicago
111 South Michigan Avenue
Chicago
IL 60603-6404
Telephone: + 1 312 443 3600
www.artic.edu

Dallas Museum of Art
1717 North Harwood
Dallas
TX 75201
Telephone: + 1 214 922 1200
www.dallasmuseumofart.org

Museum of Modern Art
11 West 53rd Street
New York
NY 10019-5497
Telephone: + 1 212 708 9400
www.moma.org

The Phillips Collection
1600 21st Street NW
Washington
DC 20009
Telephone: + 1 202 387 2151
www.phillipscollection.org

**San Francisco Museum of
Modern Art**
151 Third Street
San Francisco
CA 94103
Telephone: + 1 415 357 4000
www.sfmoma.org

**Smithsonian American Art
Museum**
1661 Pennsylvania Avenue NW
Washington
DC 20560
Telephone: + 1 202 633 2850
www.americanart.si.ed

Solomon R. Guggenheim Museum
1071 Fifth Avenue (at 89th Street)
New York
NY 10128-0173
Telephone: + 1 212 423 3500
www.guggenheim.org/new-york

abstract art
Art with no recognisable subject matter from the real world.

abstraction
Art that distorts recognisable subject matter so it doesn't look real.

acrylic paint
Paint made with pigment and manmade resin. It was invented in the 1950s, can be mixed with water, dries quickly and is now used widely by artists.

allegory
Something with a hidden symbolic meaning.

automatism
The same as free association, the method used by Freud to explore the unconscious mind of his patients. By creating when the mind was clear of all conscious thoughts, automatism was believed to explore artists' unconscious minds.

avant-garde
Artists who pioneer new approaches and methods in art.

body colour
Paint with a thick consistency or 'body', distinct from a tint or wash which is usually thin and transparent.

capitalism
An economic system, which recognises individual rights and privately owned property so individuals can generate their own profits and create their own wealth.

cast
A sculpture produced from a mould; a method of making an exact copy of an original sculpture.

collage
Technique of sticking paper, fabric and other materials on to a picture surface.

colour wheel
Circular diagram of the spectrum used to show the relationships between the colours.

commission
Fee paid to an artist to produce a work of art.

complementary colours
Two colours on opposite sides of the colour wheel, which when placed next to each other make both appear brighter.

composition
The combination of elements in a painting or other work of art so they meet the artist's requirements.

concept
An idea.

contemporary
Something that happens at that particular time or a current style.

décollage
Refers to the cutting up or tearing at parts of an original image. The French word 'décollage' translates into English as 'take-off' or 'to become unstuck'.

diptych
A painting or relief in two parts

emulsion
A fairly thin consistency, water-based paint that dries matte, smooth and opaque.

figurative art
Art that includes recognisable things; also called representational art.

fine art
Art made for itself and not for a practical purpose.

found object
An object that an artist has literally found, such as a piece of wood, bottle, ticket stub that they exhibit as a piece of art or incorporate into a work of art.

fresco
A method of painting on a wall that has just been covered in fresh plaster, before the plaster has dried properly, so the paint actually sinks in to the wall.

frottage
Technique of laying a piece of paper on a textured surface and rubbing over it with a pencil or pen to pick up the textured marks; French for 'rubbing'.

gestural painting
Describes artists' expressive individual paint marks, particularly those of the Abstract Expressionists, showing their feelings, aims and personalities.

gouache
Thick, opaque water-soluble paint, like poster paint.

graffiti
Is the plural word for 'scratch' in Italian. The practice of graffiti usually means to scratch, write or paint on property. It can be seen as a form of art or as an act of vandalism. During the 1970s, graffiti in New York subways became acknowledged as an art form.

ground
The surface on which a painter paints.

harmonising
Well-balanced colours.

impasto
Thickly applied oil paint.

kitsch
Trashy or bad taste.

lacquer
A glossy liquid taken from the lacquer tree, used as a smooth surface coating for many works of art. It can be clear or coloured.

limited palette
A restricted number of colours used in a painting.

marouflage
To stick linen or canvas to a wooden panel or plastered wall to strengthen it while preserving its texture (from a French word originally describing sticky, drying bits of paint).

materialism
Wanting wealth and material possessions without caring about moral or spiritual matters.

mixed media
Any combination of materials used in an artwork, such as watercolour and pastels or prints with added paint.

movements
In art, when a group of artists share ideas and methods at the same time.

mural
Usually large paintings on walls.

naïve art
Describes the work of artists who reject sophisticated styles in favour of childlike simplicity.

GLOSSARY

negative space
The space around or between objects rather than the objects themselves.

painterly
Qualities related to a painter's techniques in applying paint; usually with a thick, rough surface texture, as opposed to neat and precise application.

palette
A board or plate on which artists mix their paints, but also the term to describe the range of colours used by an artist.

perspective
A system of representing the three-dimensional world on a two-dimensional surface using lines, scale and colours to create the illusion of depth.

pigments
Powdered colours to be mixed with oil, water, resin or other substances to make paint.

print
An image made by taking an impression from something else. There are several types of printing that artists use, including etching, linocuts, screen prints and woodcuts.

readymade
The name given by Marcel Duchamp to a man-made object that is chosen by an artist to be exhibited as a work of art in its own right.

relief
An image with a raised surface.

resin
A sticky clear or translucent, yellow or brown substance, often used in the making of varnish, ink, glue and some plastics.

representational art
Also known as figurative art, images that look like things in the real world.

silicon
A tough synthetic material.

simultanism
A term invented by Robert Delaunay to describe the painting style he developed with his wife from about 1910, deriving from 'the law of simultaneous contrast'.

still life
A painting or arrangement of objects that do not move, such as vegetables, fruit, bones or pots.

synaesthesia
When one type of sensation provokes another sense, for example, when a sound or word triggers the sensation of a colour in the mind's eye.

tempera
Any liquid or semi-liquid mixed with powdered pigment to bind it together to make paint; usually refers to egg tempera, which is egg mixed with powdered pigment.

theosophy
Emerging in the late 19th century, Theosophy was a theory initiated by Helena Blavatsky (1831–1891), claiming that all religions are attempts by the 'Spiritual Hierarchy' to help humanity evolve and develop. Artists who became involved in the theories during the 20th century were interested in creating art that had a higher purpose than merely representing nature.

triptych
A painting or relief on three panels.

vellum
Traditional vellum is a paper-like surface made from animal skin.

INDEX

Artists' copyright
Works are copyright to the artist or the
artist's estate unless otherwise stated

© ADAGP/ FAAG, Paris and DACS, London
2009 p.27 (left)

© ADAGP, Paris and DACS, London 2009
pp.7 (left), 10, 12, 17, 19, 22, 23 (top), 23
(bottom), 27 (right), 34, 39 (top), 48, 50, 63,
66, 76, 78, 84, 94 (left)

© ARS, NY and DACS, London 2009 p.91
(bottom)

© The Estate of Francis Bacon. All rights
reserved. DACS 2009 p.99 (left)

© Bowness, Hepworth Estate p.68 (left)
and back cover

© Anthony Caro/ Barford Sculptures Ltd p.86

© DACS 2009 pp.33 (top), 36, 37, 39 (bottom
right), 46, 47, 50 (left), 50 (right), 53, 58 (left),
61 (top), 72, 73, 74, 79, 87 (right), 89 (bottom),
109 (left)

© Gala-Salvador Dalí Foundation, DACS,
London 2009 p.67 (bottom)

© Succession Marcel Duchamp/ADAGP, Paris
and DACS, London p.49 and front cover

© Tracey Emin. All rights reserved, DACS
2009 p.107

Naum Gabo © Nina Williams p.45 (right)

© Andy Goldsworthy, Courtesy Galerie
Lelong, New York p.92

© Richard Hamilton. All rights reserved,
DACS 2009 p.80

© Damien Hirst. All rights reserved,
DACS 2009 p.105 bottom

© David Hockney p.101 and front cover

© Jasper Johns/ VAGA, New York/ DACS,
London 2009 p.82

© Judd Foundation. Licensed by VAGA,
New York/ DACS, London 2009 p.89 (top)

© L & M Services B.V. The Hague 20090513
pp.16, 42 (left and right)

© The Estate of Roy Lichtenstein/ DACS
2009 p.9 (bottom)

© Succession H Matisse/ DACS 2009 pp.24,
25 and front cover

© Mario Merz by SIAE p.95 (bottom)

© Succession Miró/ ADAGP, Paris and DACS,
London 2009 p.67 (top)

Reproduced by permission of The Henry
Moore Foundation p.68 (right)

© Munch Museum/ Munch – Ellingsen
Group, BONO, Oslo/ DACS, London p.32

© Georgia O'Keeffe Museum p.71

© Succession Picasso/ DACS 2009 pp.15,
29 (right), 30, 31, 75

© The Pollock-Krasner Foundation ARS, NY
and DACS, London 2009 p.77 (top)

© Bridget Riley 2009. All rights reserved.
Courtesy Karsten Schubert London pp.18,
85 and back cover

© 2009, Banco de Mexico Diego Rivera &
Frida Kahlo Museums Trust, Mexico D F/
DACS pp.61 (bottom), 62

© 1998 Kate Rothko Prizel & Christopher
Rothko ARS, NY and DACS, London p.77
(bottom)

© Estate of Robert Smithson/ DACS,
London/ VAGA, New York 2009 p.93 (top)

© The Estate of Stanley Spencer 2009. All
rights reserved DACS p.57 (bottom)

© Tate 2009 pp.9 (top), 40

© The Andy Warhol Foundation for the
Visual Arts/ Artists Rights Society (ARS),
New York/ DACS, London 2009 pp.81, 83

Photo credits
Images were supplied by the owner of the
work unless otherwise stated

© 2004. Photo Austrian Archive/ Scala,
Florence p.21 (right)

Photograph by Robert Hashimoto © The Art
Institute of Chicago p.61 (top)

Kunstmuseum Basel, Martin P Bühler p.35

© 2009. BI, ADAGP, Paris/ Scala, Florence
p.94 (left)

British Museum, London/ Bildarchiv Foto
Marburg/ The Bridgeman Art Library p.36

© Photo CNAC/ MNAM, Dist. RMN / Droits
reserves p.63

Photo: Prudence Cuming Associates p.105
(bottom)

© Staatliche Kunstsammlungen Dresden/
The Bridgeman Art Library p.73

Courtesy of Gagosian Gallery p.104

© Imperial War Museum, London/ The
Bridgeman Art Library p.57 (bottom)

Photo: Jeanne-Claude p.91 (top left)

Walter Klein, Düsseldorf p.37

© 2009. Digital image, The Museum of
Modern Art, New York/ Scala, Florence
pp.31, 53, 54, 55 (top), 59 (right), 70, 82

Photograph by Vahida Ramujkic p.110

© 2005. Photo Schalkwijk/ Art Resource/
Scala, Florence p.61 (bottom)

Richard Schmidt p.101 and front cover

Art & Artefacts Division, Schomburg Centre
for Research in Black Culture, The New York
Public Library, Lenox and Tilden
Foundations p.65 (bottom)

© 2006. Smithsonian American Art Museum/
Art Resource/ Scala, Florence p.65 (top)

Photo: George Steinmetz p.91 (top left)

Moderna Museet, Stockholm p.47

© Storm King Art Centre, Mountainville, New
York. Photograph by Jerry L Thompson p.92

© 2008. White Images/ Scala, Florence p.75

© 2007. Yale University Art Gallery/ Art
Resource/ Scala, Florence p.34

INDEX AND ACKNOWLEDGEMENTS